MONADOLOGY
and
Other Philosophical Essays

The Library of Liberal Arts
OSKAR PIEST, FOUNDER

MONADOLOGY
and
Other Philosophical Essays

GOTTFRIED WILHELM VON LEIBNIZ

Translated by
PAUL SCHRECKER
and
ANNE MARTIN SCHRECKER

With an Introduction and Notes by
PAUL SCHRECKER

The Library of Liberal Arts
published by
Bobbs-Merrill Educational Publishing
Indianapolis

Gottfried Wilhelm von Leibniz: 1646–1716

First Edition
Tenth Printing—1980
Library of Congress Catalog Card Number: 65–26531
ISBN 0–672–60426–4 (pbk)

CONTENTS

PREFACE

At the time of Paul Schrecker's death, this edition of Leibniz works was not yet ready for the press. The introduction which he had planned to write especially for this volume was unwritten, the critical notes were not complete, and a few portions of the translation had not undergone a final revision. The publishers nonetheless desired to have the volume appear, and for this I am deeply grateful. The manuscript has, therefore, been completed in the following ways: The introductory essay is my revised and edited version of a previously unpublished paper written by Professor Schrecker in 1960, and read at St. John's College, Annapolis. The critical notes already prepared have been supplemented by adding notes from Professor Schrecker's translation into French of six of the nine works included in this volume. I have completed the revision of the translation, making only such alterations as seemed still to be necessary in order to achieve a smooth and readable English text without sacrifice of accuracy.

In completing the manuscript, I have had generous and invaluable assistance from colleagues. My expression of gratitude for their help is far more than a gesture; the edition could not have been completed without it. To Mr. M. A. Stewart I am particularly indebted for assistance in polishing the English of the two fragments on logic without distorting the meaning of the Latin text. I am deeply indebted to Professor Robert E. Butts for further assistance with the translation of the logic fragments and for suggestions concerning the bibliography, and to Professors Peter Angeles, Irving Block, and John W. Davis for help on the critical apparatus. To the University of Western Ontario, and primarily to Principal D. G. G. Kerr of Middlesex College, I express my appreciation for making available the services of a highly competent typist to prepare the final draft of the manuscript.

A. M. S.

June 1965

THE UNITY OF LEIBNIZ'
PHILOSOPHIC THOUGHT

Throughout the numerous fields of Leibniz' activity—from mathematics to metaphysics, from geology to engineering, from politics to theology, from physics and chemistry to economics, from history to linguistics—there runs a pervasive inner unity, which must be grasped for a full understanding of his work. The task of approaching this inner unity is an extremely arduous one, however, for two reasons. First of all, Leibniz never systematically exhibited it in his writings. It must, therefore, be reconstructed out of numberless fragments. For two and a half centuries Leibniz' editors have classified—and often arbitrarily —these *disjecta membra* into separate collections, frequently publishing only what they thought they understood. The result is that some two-thirds of his writings are still unpublished. The second source of the difficulty lies precisely in the multiplicity and variety of Leibniz' interests, which impose upon any adequate interpretation the duty of searching for the hidden unity of his thought, not within the domain of any one of the specialized and departmentalized scientific pursuits, but in the general idea of knowledge which dominates every particular science and constitutes the fundamental unity of the intellectual globe.

As a postulate, this universality which is more than mere consistency was the ideal of scientific work from the Renaissance to the Encyclopedists and received lip-service from the time of Francis Bacon on. In fact, since Aristotle, no one except Leibniz has taken it to be the supreme law of the Republic of Letters. For Leibniz alone was this postulated unity the motive—and the strongest one—of his multitude of achievements. The clearest evidence of this motive is found in his plan for a general science and a universal characteristic, to which he devoted work from his adolescence until his death. Unfortunately, but understandably, this gigantic plan is extant only in the form of fragments, outlines, and drafts, few of which have been published. In the context of this plan, all Leibniz' fundamental ideas find not only their determined place, but their veritable significance. It is completely erroneous to consider this idea the more or less utopian dream of a rationalist. In truth it is the indispensable basis of all the ideas we are wont to consider as eminently Leibnizian: the infinitesimal analysis and the theory of minute perceptions, the monadologic metaphysics and the dynamic laws of the shock of bodies, the new kind of formal logic and the pacifistic projects in politics and in religion. All these theories and doctrines are but applications of the method of the characteristic universal language to special problems.

There is no way to make this fundamental idea of Leibniz more adequately understood than by considering his response to the objections which Descartes had opposed to similar undertakings. In a letter to Mersenne, Descartes had maintained the impossibility of a universal language by arguing that *the invention of this language depends upon the true philosophy*. Leibniz admitted this objection—with the significant restriction *"but it does not depend upon its completion."*

To exemplify this paradoxical and somewhat cryptic assertion, one need only refer to elementary arithmetic. This science, indeed, depends entirely on a characteristic language or symbolism which is able to designate the infinity of possible numbers by a very limited set of ideographic signs—ten, in the decimal system. As Leibniz has pointed out, it can even be done with only two—one and zero—and our modern computers, anticipated by Leibniz in the one he himself invented, in fact use only two. Once this symbolism is established, the art of arithmetical calculation becomes simply the art of combining these few signs according to certain established rules of operation, without having to recur to intuition or to imagining corresponding numbers of objects. These rules are valid even for handling numbers which exceed by far the possibility of any intuitive or imaginative representation. Yet the characteristic language of arithmetic, while depending upon the "true arithmetic," that is, upon valid rules for the combination of its signs, does not in any way depend upon its completion—that is, upon the complete and explicit knowledge of all possible numbers. On the contrary, without this characteristic language it would be impossible to progress toward actualizing the completeness which is implicitly contained in its rules. How is this possible? It is possible because the whole series of integers is the result of a movement of thought. And this movement continuously adds unit to unit, collecting at each step all the past process in a higher unit; through this synthetic operation thought *creates* the series of integers. The element of this process is not the unit, but the successive addition of the unit. This is the element whose symbol is the *1* which, therefore, together with the *0*, is sufficient to produce the whole series.

Not only was the technique of the universal language of arithmetic well known to Descartes; he had, in fact, enlarged its field of application by relating algebra to geometry in such a way that the former becomes the characteristic language of the latter. Starting from geometrical intuition and symbolizing its elements by algebraic signs, he released an immense progress of both mathematical disciplines—an advancement which is due to the liberation of mathematical thought from the shackles of intuition and imagination or, differently expressed, to the possibility of formal rules of operation for the elements of extension—a general *algorism*.

Yet, even the advancement of the mathematical sciences through Descartes' analytic geometry—an advancement which can hardly be overrated, since it is presupposed by both Leibniz and Newton—was not sufficiently great to solve the central problem upon which mathematicians' efforts had converged through the centuries past: the rectification and quadrature of curvilinear figures. In this respect, Descartes is to Leibniz and Newton what Euclid had been to Apollonius of Perga and to Archimedes. It is in this context and at this point in the development of mathematics that we must place Leibniz' great invention— the infinitesimal method. Yet, this method is but the application to a special problem of his universal characteristic, just as Des-

cartes' geometry is but a specimen of the general method proposed in his *Rules for the Direction of the Mind* and his
Discourse on Method.

From the time of Archimedes, at the latest, and through the
work of such great mathematicians as Nicolaus of Cusa, Kepler,
Cavalieri, Fermat, and Pascal, curves had always been regarded
as ready-made, static figures, with directions, at best, for the construction of some of them—the so-called geometrical figures (the
circle, ellipse, parabola, hyperbola, and a few others). Other
curves, such as the line formed by a chain suspended on both
ends or by a sail into which the wind blows—the mechanical
or transcendent curves—had been declared by Descartes to be
forever inaccessible to geometrical analysis. But it is precisely
this problem which is solved by Leibniz' infinitesimal method.
Instead of considering a curve as ready-made, he analyzes the
geometrical movement which traces the curve from one point to
the infinitesimally distant next point, and develops in algebraic
symbols the rule of this movement. This mathematical dynamism had been prepared, of course, by Leibniz' predecessors,
but the new element introduced by him is the method of what
we call the *passage to the limit*, that is, a continuous movement
of thought. Consequently, for the decomposition of a curvilinear figure into partial triangles—a method which is then
faced with the problem of the summation of certain infinite
series—Leibniz substituted the generation of the curve by a continuous movement which becomes accessible to mathematics by
means of a new characteristic and a new algorism. By many of
his contemporaries, and even by later generations, this method
has been misinterpreted as dealing with infinitely small magnitudes. If this were so, the infinitesimal method would be but an
approximation, just as was Archimedes' method of exhaustion.
In truth, the differential quotient is not at all a ratio of infinitely short lines, but a purely intellectual determination of
direction at every point. Leibniz himself explicitly protests
against the admission of infinitely small magnitudes, though
he admits that occasionally this may be a convenient *façon de
parler.*

Once the determining factor has been located in the differential quotient—Leibniz calls it *differentia sive elementum*—the method of the universal characteristic requires as an additional invention only a special algorism and appropriate symbols for the operations thereby facilitated. This is the importance of the new method. "The new analysis," Leibniz writes, "considers neither figures nor numbers, but magnitudes in general, just as does ordinary algebra." By this new algorism mathematics has been enabled to "go far beyond anything accessible to imagination." It thereby not only released an explosive bursting forth of results which verified the new method, but it promoted the accession of the machine age. I am not so sure that Leibniz would have liked this child.

Now, the infinitesimal calculus offers another illustration of the possibility, indeed the necessity, of invalidating Descartes' objection to the universal language, namely, that it depends upon the true philosophy. There is ample evidence here to support Leibniz' reply that the universal language does not depend upon the completion of the true philosophy. If mathematicians had waited to introduce a characteristic language into infinitesimal geometry until the latter was completed, they would never have come any nearer this achievement. Let me propose an illustration: The parabola is an infinite figure which, therefore, can never be known *in extenso*. Yet to express its rule of construction in a characteristic language, that is, to establish its equation and its derivative, there is no need for knowing it *in extenso*. The construction principle, expressed in the characteristic language of algebra, suffices to determine any point of it at any distance. Analogously, knowledge of the element and of the law of generation suffices to establish the complete characteristic of any continuous object the construction of which obeys a rational rule. These two requirements, therefore, are sufficient and necessary to allow the application of the characteristic universal language.

Considered as a special case of this language, infinitesimal analysis thus depends upon two fundamental principles. The first principle is a rationalist postulate which appears evident and natural in mathematics, but which Leibniz endeavors to extend to cover the entire domain of rational knowledge; the second is the principle of continuity.

The rationalist postulate which serves as principle here is this: The whole of scientific progress depends upon the emancipation of thought from the limitations of intuition and imagination. Our natural languages, which are full of ambiguities and equivocations, may be able to do this for all practical purposes, but are inadequate for pure knowledge. The process of release from imaginability begins, it may be claimed, with the beginning of deductive mathematics and is still continuing, every step forward making an advance in mathematical knowledge. The results are evident in elementary arithmetic, continue in algebra and analytic geometry, and culminate in the seventeenth-century discovery of the calculus which rationalizes the continuous space of geometry and gives rise to the purely intellectual determination of extension.

Fundamentally, this is the same method which Leibniz' dynamics opposed to Descartes' mechanics. Descartes considered extension to be the essence of the material substance and could in consequence proudly assert that all his physics was but geometry. But, Leibniz objected, extension is indifferent to movement and rest; and any material object supposes not only mere geometrical extension, but something that extends in it and which, in fact, creates the appearance of extension. This something which underlies the appearance of the sensible world of bodies he called a *force*, and distinguished two aspects of it: the passive force which accounts for the impenetrability and inertia of bodies, and the active force or entelechy which engenders movement. By this means, extension as a datum of sensible perception, as well as the phenomena of elasticity, impenetrability, and movement, are reduced to one and the same rational determination. The analogy with the infinitesimal method is obvious. For henceforth the laws of physical movement, which differ from the laws of geometrical movement precisely by the intervention of forces, are nothing else but the rules of combination of elementary forces. It is possible to deduce the form of these laws adopted by Leibniz from these general principles. And, indeed, he did not base them on experience, but derived them a priori, together with the principle of conservation of *vis viva*, its correct estimation, and many other results.

Now let us consider how Leibniz applies the same principles in some very different fields. One application is his theory of "minute perceptions," that is, sensorial stimuli which are so weak or so indistinct, or occur in such great numbers simultaneously, that they do not cross the threshold of consciousness but remain, as we should say today, unconscious or subconscious. Yet these minute perceptions are not nothing; otherwise even the greatest accumulation of them would be unable to produce an assignable degree of perception. There is evidently a continuity of degree between these minute perceptions and the clear, distinct, and fully conscious perception which Leibniz calls apperception. The analogy between these minute perceptions at which you arrive by the same method of passage to the limit by which you proceed from extended magnitudes to the derivative is evident, I think: They are not at all perceptions which you might intuit, as you see or imagine short lines. Their intensity lies below any assignable degree, though they are not nothing. They are purely intellectual determinations of consciousness, building up our actual consciousness from infinitesimal and continuously added elements, the same elements which have to be postulated also for what we call—wrongly, according to Leibniz—inanimate objects.

This last remark leads us directly to the *Monadology*. The entire metaphysical system presented there represents the most profound and comprehensive application of the infinitesimal method. If it is not interpreted in this sense, it can hardly claim to be more than a sort of Platonic myth. But it is permissible, for systematic purposes, to strip the concept of the monad of its mythological trimmings. These trimmings it partly inherited from its ancestors in the history of philosophy, and partly put on to serve the purpose for which the work (an untitled writing, to which later editors gave the title *Monadology)* was *written.*

What remains after this removal of mythology is the rational determination of an individual existence as a derivative of the infinite course of the universe in space and time. Leibniz himself calls the monad a living mirror of the universe, and insists that every moment of its development contains its whole past and is pregnant with its entire future, so that we may conclude that every moment in the monad's life virtually represents the totality of the universe past, present, and future. This, indeed, appears to be rather a lofty dream than the systematic metaphysics of a consummate logician and mathematician; many interpreters of Leibniz' philosophy have therefore rashly relegated it to a place among his alleged attempts to win popularity. Let me attempt to show how groundless this accusation is, particularly if the monadologic system is not interpreted solely from the writing which circulates under the name *Monadology*, but from the many writings of Leibniz' mature period, chiefly those written in Latin.

The differential quotient of any curve, you will remember, can be derived from its analytic equation. It follows therefrom that any infinitesimal part of the curve contains virtually the entire curve, even though, like a parabola or a hyperbola, the curve may be infinite. Moreover, the movement which traces the curve according to the law expressed in the derivative is not a process in time, but a logical process: All the points of the curve are simultaneous, or rather, there is no time relation between them any more than there is between the premises and conclusion of a syllogism, although our discursive understanding thinks them successively. Interpreting the monadology after this mathematical model, we may first say something concerning the succession of the monad's states, each of which follows the preceding with autonomous necessity, that is, without any interference from anything else. But is not this development, this conation from one perception to the next, a process in time? Here lies an important point which has very rarely been observed. Certainly Leibniz often speaks as though it were such a process, but if you take his remarks literally, you will find yourself faced with an inconsistency in his philosophy. For whenever he deals with the problem of time, he considers it as a mere order of phenomena, not endowed with any ontological status. And furthermore, he asserts in many of his more esoteric works, particularly in the *Ultimate Origination of the Universe,* that the universe before creation was, in its infinite totality, an idea in the divine mind. This implies that God, who does not think discursively, conceived simultaneously all the monads with all their infinite developments. And since no other kind of thought is possible for God than intellectual, or rational, intuition, the relations of the empirically successive states of the monads must be rational, although *we* know them only empirically, in a temporal succession. Just as the mathematician virtually knows all the points of a curve if and when he knows its derivative, without tracing the figure on paper and without recurring to imagination; just as the architect has an adequate knowledge of a building when he looks at the blueprints, without needing to see it developed in space; so the supreme architect and mathematician knows the universe adequately because he knows the reason why it is such as it is and not different: in other words, because he knows the laws according to which it is going to operate. These laws, needless to add, are rational, however arbitrary and contingent they may appear to us.

Another isomorphism of the monadology with the mathematical model of the calculus may become clear as we consider the second of the principles upon which infinitesimal analysis depends, the *principle of continuity.* The principle of continuity, according to Leibniz, is a rational principle a priori which could not possibly be derived from experience nor proved by inductive reasoning, but is a universal principle of order, that is, of general science. Popularly expressed, the principle states that nature makes no leaps; in this form it antedates Leibniz by many centuries. But it is a more precise and not at all anthropomorphic formulation which is proposed by Leibniz in his more technical works. "When two hypothetical conditions," he writes, for instance, in his *Critical Remarks on Descartes' Principles,* "or two different data continuously approach each other until finally the one of them passes into the other, then

necessarily also the results sought or the effects of both conditions must continuously approach each other and the one finally
must disappear into the other and vice versa." If we are attempt-
ing to understand nature scientifically, we are obliged to assume
that it is susceptible of being ordered according to this principle,
for otherwise any rational analysis and in consequence any
mathematical science of nature would be impossible. While the
first application of the principle is in mathematics itself, where
it supports the infinite divisibility of extension and number,
and thereby the irrational numbers and the method of the
passage to the limit, its further application stretches far beyond
and comprehends all sciences, including metaphysics, biology,
history, and linguistics. The laws of motion and of the collision
of bodies, which—due to the passage to the limit—also cover
the state of rest, that is, of movement the velocity of which is
smaller than any assignable quantity; the obliteration of the
opposition of life and death, animate and inert matter, which
is familiar to those who have studied the *Monadology*—these
and many other instances give evidence of the all-pervasive
function in Leibniz' thought of the principle of continuity—a
principle which, in its turn, secures the possibility and unity of
rational science.

Pure rationality emancipated from the limitations of imagination, and the principle of continuity thus appear as two of
the mainstays of the unity of Leibniz' thought, and especially
of his lifelong attempt toward a characteristic universal language. I have several times referred to this plan, and shall now
present it in a more detailed and specific way. Let me first explain the terms. A characteristic language is one in which there
is a one-to-one relation between an arbitrary sign or character
and the signified idea or thing, that is, in which one character
represents only one idea or thing, and one idea or thing can be
represented by only one character. In our natural languages this
is not the case, hence they are full of open or hidden ambiguities
and equivocations. A *count* may signify a nobleman or the result of numbering, and the names Great Bear and Big Dipper

stand for one and the same constellation. There may even be words which stand for nothing, such as the famous phlogiston of seventeenth-century chemistry. Consider, for instance, how many and incompatible are the ideas covered by such words as freedom, democracy, or, alas, even philosophy. There was in Leibniz' time only one field of knowledge, and that the most certain one, which used a truly characteristic language: arithmetic. If you write down the sign "5" it stands for only one idea and this idea cannot be expressed by any other single sign. You may *pronounce* it five, *cinq*, *penta*, or in as many other ways as there are natural languages, but the signified idea remains the same. In brief, this sign is an ideogram, as are also the signs for arithmetical operations, like plus, minus, or the radical sign. The same is true today for chemistry, where the symbol "K" stands for the nineteenth element, whether you call it potassium or Kalium or any other name. The chemical symbols are today agreed upon internationally, and this leads us to the second qualification of Leibniz' philosophical language, namely, that it be universal, independent of any national language. How did he expect to invent such a language which would be able not only to express all rational truths, but even to find them, to function as the true *ars inveniendi*, which Descartes believed he had discovered in algebra? By means of this *scientia mirabilis* Descartes had expected to embrace in one single system all the sciences of nature, reduced to algebraic formulas. His expectation, however, remained a methodological program or, rather, a program for a methodology; in fact, not a single equation appeared in his physics. Leibniz realized that one of the reasons for this shortcoming was the identification of mechanics with geometry, which rendered Descartes unable to account for that element of the laws of nature which is not geometric but, as Leibniz called it, architectonic. Descartes had considered algebra to be the universal science, of which arithmetic and geometry are but the *integuments*, as he called them, the covering skins. Leibniz, on the other hand, conceived the idea of a genuinely universal science, in relation to which not only the mathematical and physical sciences, including algebra, but metaphysics and jurisprudence as well, were to be mere integuments. And while Descartes' universal science was essentially a method of demonstration for deductive sets of theorems, Leibniz' universal science was to become, not merely a method of demonstration, but a method of invention and discovery, aiming not only at deductive certainty, but just as much at estimating probabilities. How did he conceive this to become possible? Let me briefly sketch the procedure he had in view.

Suppose we had an encyclopedia of all human knowledge. Then we could collect all the words used in it, define them adequately, then define the words used in these definitions, until we came upon undefinable primitives. The number of these primitives—of which all the other words would be but combinations, just as all the words of English are but combinations of twenty-six letters—would certainly remain far below the number of words recorded in the dictionary of the language in which the encyclopedia is written, just as there is an infinity of integers which yet need only two signs, *1* and *0,* to be adequately and characteristically symbolized.

The next step is to find suitable signs for these primitives. Then all that remains to be done is to develop the syntax of this new characteristic language, that is, rules of operation for the combination of these signs, an algorism of symbols, which would have the same unerring certainty as the algorisms of arithmetic, which a machine can perform more reliably and economically than the human mind. This new algorism would achieve without reasoning the effect of reasoning; and, henceforth, if two scientists disagreed, they would say: Let us sit down and calculate. How seriously Leibniz took this project and how deeply rooted it was in his thought may be evidenced by a few observations. At the age of twenty (in 1666) he published a dissertation *De arte combinatoria (On the Combinatory Art)*, a mathematical–logical investigation of the formal algorisms of combinatories. Second, among his papers preserved in the Library of Hanover we have found thick files filled with hundreds of pages of definitions, collected for the purpose of arriving at the undefinable primitives. Thirdly, Leibniz was

THE UNITY OF LEIBNIZ' PHILOSOPHIC THOUGHT

well aware of the fact that in his time specialization was already raising its ugly head and that it would be far beyond the capacity of any one scholar to compile the encyclopedia which is a necessary step toward the characteristic language; it would therefore have to issue from the cooperative efforts of many specialists. This and nothing else was the motive of his relentlessly pursued plan for the foundation of academies in the principal centers of learning—Berlin, Leipzig, Vienna, Petersburg, and elsewhere. Only one of these, the Prussian Academy of the Sciences in Berlin, was founded during his lifetime; he became its first president. The others followed soon after his death, and if they did not live up to his expectations, it was not his fault. At any rate, they have ever since their founding functioned as cooperative enterprises, and never have been mere imitations of similar older institutions in other countries—as the Royal Society in London, the French Academy in Paris, or the still much older Italian academies. And finally, among Leibniz' papers in Hanover there are thousands of manuscript pages, very many of them unpublished, dating back to his thirties, covered with the record of his unwavering efforts toward two goals: the invention of a suitable symbolism for the primitives, and the invention of operational rules for the combination of these primitives. That he attained his goal in neither respect by no means diminishes the merit of his efforts. It must be kept in mind that even today the signs for the primitives of formal logic are not universally agreed upon and still undergo rather rapid change. As to the rules of operation, or what is today called formal logic or logical calculus, they are still far from being universal. And this despite the historical fact that the contemporary development of formal logic has been inestimably facilitated by the invention of Cantorian set theory (in the 1880's)— facilitated, yet again, by an advance in mathematics.

A brief consideration of Leibniz' work in the practical fields of politics and religion will serve to show that here, too, the unity of his thought and of his method remains unbroken. I have earlier stressed the conciliatory or pacifistic character of his thought. In philosophy it manifests itself, for instance, in his contention that there is some degree of truth in every system—each one, one-sided as it may be, being but truth represented from a particular viewpoint, just as every monad represents the same universe from a certain viewpoint and, therefore, inadequately. Only all the monads together would represent it adequately, if an integration of their views were possible. It would not be the least important function of the characteristic language to replace the eternal feuds and quarrels of schools with rational calculation. The same attitude determines Leibniz' lifelong attempts to bring about the reunion and union of the Christian churches. Born two years before the end of the Thirty Years' War, he had witnessed all the misery and desolation caused by religious intolerance and division; this condition did not end with the Peace of Westphalia but continued to ravage the Europe of his time. Catholics against Protestants, Calvinists against Lutherans—these were not merely theological controversies, but the tinder for ever-renewed wars and atrocious persecutions. Now wars are, of all human follies and bestialities, the most irrational, and hence cannot be the will of God. There can be only one true religion which the various churches perceive from various viewpoints, each one containing some truth and more error. What can be done about this? Leibniz' idea was to analyze the tenets in which the several creeds disagreed and to find out whether the differences were real or merely verbal. To that end he expended an immense amount of historical and theological research to clarify the two most controversial issues, namely, predestination and transubstantiation. What he found was that the churches really quarreled about words or about irrelevant ritual conventions, and that rationally there was no essential divergence among the Christian denominations. His optimism may have overlooked the many irrational elements of civilization which have caused or at least reinforced religious divisions. Yet for a time his heroic fight did not appear quixotic; some progress actually was made, only to be stifled in 1706 by the intervention of power politics. Even then Leibniz' rational optimism did not surrender: "Some day," he wrote to a friend, "this thing—the union—will actualize itself spontaneously."

Similar basic ideas pervade Leibniz' political philosophy also, though at the same time he was a successful politician and diplomat whose contributions to the rise of his ducal house of Hanover to the Electorate and their later accession to the British throne are by no means negligible. In 1693 he published a big volume in-folio under the title: *Codex juris gentium diplomaticus* (*A Diplomatic Code of International Law*), followed ten years later by a second part. This book is by no means a code as we understand the word. It is a collection of international treaties and similar documents which date back to the tenth century. According to Leibniz they clearly evince the validity of certain patterns of international law which, without ever having been legislated or expressly agreed upon, have yet been tacitly accepted as ruling international relations and distinguishing legal from illegal actions. Here again we see his principle of infinitesimal method at work. It would be vain to enact a complete code of international law. What can be done, however, is to study the historical movement apparently and gradually increasing its sway through numberless minute accretions which finally, he believed, will accumulate to form an extended reign of law in that domain which is most exclusively dominated by the irrational factors of passions and power. In the Preface to his *Code*, he has formulated the basic rational principles which would have to inspire such a future system of international law. Variations, in fact, of principles of Stoic ethics adopted by the great Roman jurists, perhaps even tautological, they nevertheless clearly express norms without which no rational system of law can exist. They are simply: Harm no one; Give everyone what is his; Live honestly.

How could Leibniz, despite all experience to the contrary, justify his belief in rationality and its practical aspect, justice? For him the universe is an idea of God, to which creation has added actuality. And since the divine wisdom which conceived the plan of the universe differs from our reason only by degree, and not in essence, this plan must be rational, although fre-

quently the reasons necessarily escape limited spirits such as
we are. Hence, the postulate of rationality and the principle of
continuity, which express an intrinsic quality of the rational
universe, must be accepted in order to decode the cryptogram
to which science attempts to discover the key. Once this key—
the rational elements of reality plus the rules of their combination—has been discovered, its application in a characteristic
universal language could overcome our limitation, just as the
invention of the arithmetical signs and of their algorism has
overcome the limitation of our imagination. This theological
foundation of the intelligibility of the universe plays, in the
philosophy of Leibniz, the same role as the veracity of God in
that of Descartes. It is in fact but the translation into metaphysical language of the hypothesis which lies hidden at the
foundation of all science, namely, that scientific knowledge
presupposes an object susceptible of being ordered by rational
thought.

Modern science has been able to follow Leibniz only in proportion to its readiness to open its gates to mathematics and
to logic. But the very possibility of applying these sciences a
priori to reality depends upon the fundamental ideas of Leibniz
which I have tried to epitomize here. In this direction, as recent
stages of the history of science clearly manifest, the effective
influence of these ideas is far from exhausted.

PAUL SCHRECKER

NOTES ON THE TEXTS

One may consider it a general rule that Leibniz wrote in Latin the books and the philosophic and scientific treatises destined for the restricted public of savants, and in French those by which he desired to attract the more extended circle composed of the *honnêtes gens* of his time. This rule, of course, suffers some exceptions, which can be explained either by the place of publication or by the nationality of the person to whom the writing is particularly addressed. In general, however, it can be stated that when a subject has been treated by Leibniz in the two languages, the Latin version is more concise, more rigorous, more difficult reading, in a more esoteric language; while the French version is more easily accessible to the larger public, better suited to popularize and to spread the new ideas of the author.

Thus it is necessarily to the Latin works of Leibniz that we must have recourse for a more precise and more profound knowledge of his work. With the exception of the *Monadology*, the works translated for this volume were written in Latin. Our choice of works has as its purpose, on the one hand, to present reliable texts and faithful translations of several writings indispensable to the study and understanding of the Leibnizian philosophy, and on the other hand, to permit the reader to follow this thought in certain decisive steps of its development. All the translations presented here are new. The texts used were those of the *Philosophische Schriften* published by C. I. Gerhardt (7 vols.; Berlin, 1875–1890). For the works printed during Leibniz' lifetime, these texts have been collated with those of the first edition; that is to say, with the *Acta eruditorum* of Leipzig for the works first published there, and for the *Causa Dei*, with the original edition (as an appendix to the *Théodicée*) published in Amsterdam by Isaac Troyel in 1710. The text of the *De rerum originatione radicali* has been collated with the manuscript in Hanover.

The *Meditationes de cognitione, veritate et ideis (Reflections on Knowledge, Truth, and Ideas)*, published for the first time in the *Acta eruditorum* in November 1684, constitute the first writing properly classified as philosophical that Leibniz published after his return from Paris in 1676, and at the same time the opening work in his long polemic against Descartes and the Cartesians. One does not yet find, however, the exposition of the points of doctrine on which his opposition to the Cartesians will be the most vehement and the most irreducible, namely, his theory of the active essence of matter and his dynamism.

It is the *Animadversiones in partem generalem principiorum Cartesianorum (Critical Remarks Concerning the General Part of Descartes' Principles)* which develops these theories in the most explicit and lucid fashion, by following Descartes' text itself, paragraph by paragraph. We know, from the correspondence of Leibniz with Basnage de Beauval, that this work was written in 1692, that the author wished to publish it with the work of Descartes which it claimed to refute, and that the publishing houses of both Germany and Holland refused to undertake the edition. Until 1697 Leibniz unsuccessfully pursued this project, and even began to revise the manuscript—the variants are to be found in the Gerhardt edition. However, the work did not appear until 1844, when it was published by G. E. Guhrauer. This is perhaps the work of Leibniz which permits the easiest access to his dynamics and reveals most clearly the close relations of the dynamics to the metaphysics. Unfortunately, it is relatively little known.

The little dissertation *De primae philosophiae emendatione, et de notione substantiae (On the Improvement of Metaphysics, and on the Concept of Substance)*, published for the first time in the *Acta eruditorum* of 1694, is less a methodical exposition than the program or the succinctly rendered account of the investigations of the author into a fundamental problem of metaphysics. One finds here the ideas which Leibniz had already formulated in two articles in the *Journal des savants*, June 1691 and January 1693 (Gerhardt, IV, pp. 464–467).

De rerum originatione radicali (On the Ultimate Origination of the Universe), written in November 1697, was published only in 1840, after the manuscript of Hanover, in the Erdmann edition. There is, in Gerhardt, VII, pp. 289–291, and in the *Opuscules et fragments inédits de Leibniz,* published by L. Couturat (Paris, 1903), pp. 533–535, an outline or highly condensed resumé of this treatise. A central idea of this text, the close connection between teleology and mechanism, recalls in a striking fashion a passage of the *Timaeus* (48a) of Plato, which presents wisdom as persuading necessity to bring the greatest number of things to the greatest possible perfection.

De ipsa natura (What Is Nature?) appeared for the first time in the *Acta eruditorum* of September 1698. Leibniz himself reveals here the circumstances which had led him to the discussion of this topic with one of the most important representatives of Cartesianism in Germany. The philosophy of the author appears here as already closely approaching the definitive form which it will take in the *Monadology*. One of the guiding ideas of Leibniz' thought, the conciliation of the Cartesian mechanism with the traditional philosophy of Platonic and Aristotelian inspiration, is expressly stated at the end of this work.

The *Causa Dei (A Vindication of God's Justice)*, published as an appendix to the *Théodicée* in 1710, summarizes in a rigorous and concise style the development of ideas in the great work in which Leibniz explains his position on the subject of the theological skepticism of Pierre Bayle. Born of discourses addressed to the Queen of Prussia on problems treated in Bayle's *Dictionnaire historique et critique,* the *Théodicée* is much more a highly popularized work than a methodical and formal exposition of the Leibnizian theology. That is why Leibniz, recognizing that the *Théodicée* was not a scientific work but only a "web" of thoughts, expressed "a bit colloquially," added to it a systematic abridgment in Latin directed more particularly xxviiiNOTES ON THE TEXTS

to theologians and philosophers. Forty years of struggle for the union of the churches, divided above all on the very questions discussed in this work, had matured the theology of Leibniz, which has found here an expression both lucid and permeated with wisdom.

P. S.

SELECTED BIBLIOGRAPHY

Principal Editions of Leibniz' Works

Sämtliche Schriften und Briefe. Edited by the Deutschen Akademie der Wissenschaften. Darmstadt and Leipzig, 1923—. This edition is planned as a complete and critical edition. The following volumes have appeared: I, *Politischer und historischer Briefwechsel,* Vols. I-V. II, *Philosophischer Briefwechsel,* Vol. I (1663–1684). III, *Politische Schriften,* Vol. I (1667–1676). VI, *Philosophische Schriften,* Vol. I (1663–1672).

Philosophische Schriften. Ed. C. I. GERHARDT. 7 vols. Berlin, 1875–1890.

Mathematische Schriften. Ed. C. I. GERHARDT. 7 vols. Berlin and Halle, 1849–1855.

Opera omnia. Ed. LOUIS DUTENS. 6 vols. Geneva, 1768—.

Opera philosophiae quae extant. Ed. J. E. ERDMANN, 2 vols. Berlin, 1840.

Opuscules et fragments inédits. Ed. LOUIS COUTURAT. Paris, 1903. (Papers on logic and related fields.)

English Translations

ALEXANDER, H. G. (ed.). *The Leibniz-Clarke Correspondence.* New York: Philosophical Library, 1956.

DUNCAN, G. M. (trans.). *The Philosophical Works of Leibnitz.* New Haven: Tuttle, Morehouse & Taylor, 1890, 1908.

HUGGARD, E. M. (trans.). *G. W. Leibniz: Theodicy.* Introduction by A. FARRER. New Haven: Yale University Press, 1952.

LANGLEY, A. G. (trans.). *New Essays concerning Human Understanding, by Gottfried Wilhelm Leibniz; Together with an Appendix of Some of His Shorter Pieces.* Chicago: Open Court, 1916, 1949.

LATTA, R. (trans.). *Leibniz: The Monadology and Other Philosophical Writings.* Oxford, 1898. Reprinted, London: Oxford University Press, 1925.

LOEMKER, LEROY E. (trans.). *Leibniz: Philosophical Papers and Letters.* 2 vols. Chicago: University of Chicago Press, 1956.

LUCAS, P. G., and GRINT, L. (trans.). *Leibniz, Discourse on Metaphysics.* Manchester, 1953.

MONTGOMERY, G. R. W. (trans.). *Leibniz: Discourse on Metaphysics, Correspondence with Arnauld, and Monadology.* Chicago: Open Court, 1902, 1962.

MORRIS, MARY (trans.). *The Philosophical Writings of Leibniz, Selected and Translated.* "Everyman's Library." New York: E. P. Dutton & Co., Inc., 1934.

WIENER, PHILIP (ed.). *Leibniz Selections.* "Scribner Modern Student's Library." New York, 1951.

Selected Works on Leibniz

BARBER, W. H. *Leibniz in France, from Arnauld to Voltaire. A Study in French Reactions to Leibnizianism, 1670–1760.* Oxford: Clarendon Press, 1955.

CASSIRER, ERNST. *Leibniz's System in seinen wissenschaftlichen Grundlagen.* Marburg, 1902. Reprinted, Hildesheim: G. Olms, 1962.

COUTURAT, LOUIS. *La Logique de Leibniz d'après documents inédits.* Paris, 1901. Reprinted, Hildesheim: G. Olms, 1961.

JOSEPH, H. W. B. *Lectures on the Philosophy of Leibniz.* Oxford: Clarendon Press, 1949.

RUSSELL, BERTRAND. *A Critical Exposition of the Philosophy of Leibniz.* Cambridge: University Press, 1900. 2nd ed., London: G. Allen & Unwin, 1949.

YOST, R. M. *Leibniz and Philosophical Analysis.* Berkeley: University of California Press, 1954.

MONADOLOGY
and
Other Philosophical Essays

REFLECTIONS ON KNOWLEDGE,
TRUTH, AND IDEAS

Eminent men are engaged today in a controversy regarding true and false ideas.[1] Since this problem is of great importance for the knowledge of truth, and since even Descartes has not given an entirely satisfactory solution, I have thought it appropriate to explain briefly what I think must be said on the differences and the criteria of ideas and cognitions. All knowledge is either obscure or *clear*, and clear knowledge is again either confused or *distinct*; the distinct in its turn is either inadequate or *adequate*, and again either symbolic or *intuitive*. The most perfect knowledge is that which is both adequate and intuitive.

A notion is *obscure* when it does not suffice for the recognition of the represented thing. Thus, I may have a certain recollection of some flower or animal which I have seen once, yet this recollection may not suffice for me to recognize it when it is presented to me or to distinguish it from a flower or animal which resembles it closely. This is also the case when I consider some term insufficiently explained in the Schools, e.g., Aristotle's Entelechy, or the term "cause," which may equally well designate the material, the formal, the efficient, and the final cause, and others of this kind of which we have no precise definition. Hence any proposition which uses such a term also becomes obscure.

[1] This refers to the controversy between Antoine Arnauld and Nicolas Malebranche on the origin of our ideas. It had been opened by Arnauld's book, *Des vrayes et des fausses idées contre ce qu'enseigne l'auteur de la recherche de la vérité* (*On True and False Ideas, Against the Teachings of the Author of the Search after Truth*), Cologne, 1683, to which Malebranche replied with the *Réponse de l'auteur de la recherche de la vérité au livre de M. Arnauld des vrayes et des fausses idées* (*Answer of the Author of the Search after Truth to the Book of M. Arnauld*), Rotterdam, 1684. In the last paragraph of the present article Leibniz comes back to the core of this controversy.

Knowledge is therefore *clear* when it suffices to let me recognize the represented thing; and such knowledge in its turn is either confused or distinct. It is *confused* when I am unable to enumerate separately the marks which are sufficient to distinguish this thing from others, although it actually has such required elements and marks into which the notion of it can be resolved. Thus we recognize with sufficient clearness colors, odors, tastes, and other peculiar sense objects, and can distinguish them from each other, but only through the simple testimony of the senses, not through describable marks. We are, for instance, unable to explain to a blind man what redness is; even to others we cannot explain such qualities unless we place them in the presence of the thing itself and make them see, smell, or taste it, or unless we recall to their minds certain similar sensations which they have experienced in the past. Yet it is certain that the notions of these qualities are composite and susceptible of being resolved, since each of these qualities has its cause. Similarly we see that painters and other artists recognize perfectly well what is well done and what is badly done, but are often unable to give reasons for their judgment, and answer when questioned that in the work which displeases them a certain I-know-not-what is lacking. Now, a *distinct* notion is like the one which assayers have of gold, which enables them to distinguish it from all other similar bodies by certain marks and tests. Such are, ordinarily, the notions we have of objects common to several senses, such as number, magnitude, and figure; such too are many affections of our minds, such as hope and fear, and, in short, all those notions of which we have *nominal definitions*, which are nothing else but enumerations of sufficient marks. However, distinct cognition of undefinable notions is also possible, namely, when the notion is *primitive*, that is, a mark of itself, or when it is irresolvable and can only be understood through itself, hence lacks elements. With regard to composite notions it may happen that the single notions which compose them are in their turn clearly yet confusedly known, for instance, weight, color, nitric acid, and other elements which constitute the notion of gold. This knowledge, therefore, though distinct, is still *inadequate*. But when everything which enters a distinct notion is in its turn distinctly known, that is, when the analysis is pursued to the end, then the cognition is *adequate*. I doubt whether man can give a perfect example of such knowledge; the numeral concepts come very near it. For the most part, however, and particularly when the analysis is long, we do not intuit simultaneously the whole nature of the thing; rather, we use signs instead of things, and for brevity's sake usually omit explaining them in the present chain of thoughts, knowing or believing that to give the explanation is in our power. Thus, when I think of a chiliogon (a polygon of one thousand equal sides), I do not always consider the nature of a side, of equality, and of the number one thousand (that is, the cube of ten), but use these words (the sense of which is only obscurely and imperfectly present to the mind) instead of the ideas which I have of them. For I remember that I am in possession of the signification of these words, and therefore think it unnecessary to explain them now. I am wont to call this knowledge *blind*, or *symbolic*; we use it also in algebra and in arithmetic, and almost everywhere else. Certainly when the notion is highly composite, we are unable to think at the same time all the notions which enter into it. But where this is possible, or at least insofar as it is possible, I call the knowledge *intuitive*. Of a distinct and primitive notion no other knowledge is possible than the intuitive, just as for the most part we think of component notions only by means of symbols.

Hence it becomes evident that even of distinctly known things we do not perceive the ideas unless and insofar as we use intuitive cognition. Nevertheless, it sometimes happens that we falsely believe we have in our minds the *ideas* of things because we falsely suppose that we have already explained certain terms which we are using. And it is certainly untrue or at least equivocal what certain authors affirm: that we cannot speak of a thing, understanding what we are saying, unless we have an idea of that thing.[2] For frequently we understand very well each of the

[2] This is the doctrine of Descartes. See, e.g., his letter to Mersenne, July 1641, in *Oeuvres de Descartes*, Adam-Tannery edn. (J. Vrin: Paris, 1897–1913), Vol. III, p. 393: "When we express anything by our words and understand what we are saying, it is certain by this very fact that we have in us the idea of the thing signified by our words."

words we are using or we remember having understood them before; yet because we content ourselves with this blind knowledge and do not pursue far enough the analysis of the notions, it happens that a contradiction which may be implied in the composite notion escapes us. Some time ago I was moved to a closer examination of this question by the argument, long famous among the Schoolmen and renewed by Descartes, which proves the existence of God by this syllogism: Whatever follows from the idea or definition of a thing may be predicated of the thing itself. Now, existence follows from the idea of God, since he is defined as the most perfect being or the being than which no greater can be conceived. (For the most perfect being implies all the perfections, among which belongs existence.) *Ergo*, existence can be predicated of God. But in truth it ought to be realized that from this argument only the following conclusion can be drawn: If God be possible, it follows that he exists.[3] For we cannot use definitions to draw conclusions with certainty before we know that the definitions are real, that is, that they involve no contradiction. The reason for this is that from notions implying a contradiction, opposite conclusions can simultaneously be drawn, which is absurd. To explain this I usually avail myself, as an example, of the notion of the most rapid motion, which implies an absurdity. For suppose that a wheel turns with that most rapid motion; who would not see that a spoke of that wheel extended beyond the rim will at its extremity move with greater velocity than a nail on the circumference of the wheel? Therefore, the movement of this nail is not the most rapid, which contradicts the hypothesis. Yet at first sight it may appear that we do have an idea of the most rapid motion, for we understand thoroughly what we are speaking about, while of impossible things we possess absolutely no idea. For the same reasons it does not suffice to think of the most perfect Being in order to affirm that we have an idea of it. In the demonstration referred to above, the possibility of this Being must be

---

[3] This objection had already been made by the authors of the "Second Objections" against the *Meditations* of Descartes. See Adam-Tannery, VII, 127.

proved or assumed to make the conclusion valid. Meanwhile, it is very true that we have the idea of God and that the most perfect Being is possible, nay necessary. The alleged argument, however, is not conclusive, and St. Thomas Aquinas had already rejected it.[4]

By this means we also obtain the distinction between *nominal definitions*, which contain only marks to distinguish the defined things from others, and *real definitions*, by which the possibility of the defined notion is established. Thus we take care of Hobbes, who pretended that all truths are arbitrary, because they depend on nominal definitions.[5] He did not consider, however, that the reality of a definition does not depend upon us and that not any notions whatever can be combined together. It is true that nominal definitions do not suffice for perfect knowledge unless it is established otherwise that the defined thing is possible. It is also evident therefrom which *ideas* are *true* and which *false*. An idea is true when the notion is possible and false when it involves contradiction. *Possibility* can be known either *a priori* or *a posteriori;* it is known a priori when we resolve the notion into its requisites or into other notions the possibility of which is already established, and when we find in it no incompatibility. This can be done, for instance, when we understand the way in which the thing is produced— hence the particularly great usefulness of *causal definitions*. We know the possibility a posteriori when we know by experience that the thing actually exists; for whatever actually exists or has existed is certainly possible. Whenever, then, we have adequate knowledge, we have also a priori knowledge of a possibility. For when the analysis is pursued to its end and no contradiction appears, the notion is certainly possible. However, I would not yet dare to affirm that it will ever be possible for men to perform a perfect analysis of notions, that is, to reduce their thoughts to the *first possibles* and irresolvable notions or, which comes to the same, to the absolute attributes of God themselves, which

---

[4] See for instance his *Summa contra Gentiles* I. 10.

[5] See the "Third Objections" (of Hobbes) against the *Meditations*, Adam-Tannery, VII, 178; and Hobbes' *De corpore*, Part I, chap. 3, paragraph 7.

are the first causes and ultimate reasons of all things. For the most part we content ourselves with gathering the reality of certain notions from experience and compounding them afterward into others, following the example of nature.

Hence I think it can be understood at last that the appeal to ideas is not always without danger and that many authors abuse this specious title to give some weight to certain products of their imaginations. For from the fact that we are conscious of thinking of some thing it does not follow that we have an idea of that thing, as I have shown above by the example of the motion of maximum velocity. It seems to me also that in our days men abuse no less frequently that often affirmed principle: *whatever I perceive clearly and distinctly of a thing is true and can be predicated of it.*[6] For frequently what appears to be clear and distinct to people who judge superficially is actually obscure and confused. The axiom is therefore useless, unless we add *criteria* of clearness and distinctness, as we have proposed them, and unless the truth of the ideas is established with certainty. For the rest, the rules of *common logic*—rules which are also used by the geometricians—should not be neglected as criteria for the truth of propositions. Such, for instance, is the rule that nothing ought to be admitted as certain unless proved by accurate experiment or solid demonstration. A solid demonstration is one which respects the forms prescribed by logic. It is not always necessary to argue in the classical order of syllogisms as the Schoolmen did (and as did Christian Herlin and Conrad Dasypodius in their treatment of the first six books of Euclid).[7] But it is necessary at least that the argument conclude by virtue of the form. Of such an *argument in good form*, any calculation correctly carried out offers an example. Thus, no necessary premise is to be omitted, and all premises must be either dem-

[6] See Descartes, Adam-Tannery, VII, 115, 150, 162; and Arnauld, *Port-Royal Logic*, Part IV, chap. 8.

[7] The two mathematicians of Strasburg referred to here published a Greek–Latin edition of the first six books of Euclid (Strasburg, 1564–1566). In the Latin translation and in the commentaries of the editors, all propositions are presented as conclusions of formal arguments.

onstrated beforehand or only assumed as hypotheses, in which case the conclusion also is hypothetical. If these rules are carefully observed, we shall easily avoid deceitful ideas. In his very famous dissertation on the geometrical spirit (of which a fragment is preserved in the excellent book on the art of thinking whose author is the great Antoine Arnauld), the very ingenuous Pascal has expressed much the same thing, saying that the geometrician should define all terms which are however little obscure and demonstrate all truths however little doubtful.[8] But I wish he had defined the limits beyond which a notion or proposition is no longer however little obscure or doubtful. The necessary requisites may, however, be gathered by an attentive study of what we have said in the present essay, for I must try now to be brief.

As regards the controversy whether we see all things in God (a very old doctrine which, if well understood, should not be absolutely spurned) or whether we have our own ideas,[9] it should be pointed out that even if we saw all things in God, it would still be necessary for us to have our own ideas, which are not like little images but are affections or modifications of our minds which correspond to the very same things we see in God. For certainly, as one thought succeeds another, a certain change is produced in our minds, and even the ideas of things of which we are not actually thinking at present must be in our minds, just as is the statue of Hercules in the marble block. In God,

8 A fragment of Pascal's posthumous *Ésprit géométrique* was inserted by the authors—Arnauld and Nicole—into their famous *Port-Royal Logic, or the Art of Reasoning*, of 1662.

9 The thesis that "we see all things in God" had been proposed by Malebranche in his *Recherche de la vérité* (*The Search After Truth*) of 1673–1674. Leibniz calls it "very old" because it goes back, as Malebranche recognized, to St. Augustine's doctrine that we see the truths in God. Leibniz was familiar with Malebranche's thesis, since he had read the book when it came out, during his sojourn in Paris; his interpretation of it, however, is neither accurate nor very fair. According to Malebranche, the things we see in God are the objects of mathematics, i.e., extension and number; and he himself insisted that, of these ideas, there are subjective representations—"modifications of our minds."

however, there must actually be not only the idea of absolute and infinite extension, but also of all the figures which are nothing else than modifications of absolute extension. Even when we perceive colors or odors, we are perceiving nothing else but figures and movements, but figures and movements so small, so varied, and in such great number, that our minds are not capable in their present states of considering them singly and distinctly. As a consequence we are not aware that our perceptions are composed of infinitesimally small perceptions of figures and movements. For example, when we thoroughly mix very fine yellow and blue powders, we perceive green; we are not aware that what we in fact perceive is only yellow and blue, very finely mixed, but believe rather that we see some new fictitious entity.

ON THE UNIVERSAL SCIENCE:
CHARACTERISTIC

XIV

All our certain knowledge is established through *demonstrations* or through *experiments*. In both, reason dominates. For the very *art of inventing experiments* and of using them rests on certain reasons; it does not depend upon chance or accident. Let us at present disregard experiments, which require the expenditure of money, equipment, and time, and are furthered by chance, and let us concentrate on that *improvement of the sciences* which is *based on reason*.

The advancement of the rational art of invention depends, to a large extent, upon the improvement of the art of characteristic symbols. Usually men seek demonstrative certainty only regarding numbers, lines, and the things thereby represented. The reason for this limitation is that, apart from numbers, we have no other *convenient characteristic symbols which correspond to concepts*. This is also the reason why, up to now, not even geometry has been treated analytically, except insofar as it can be reduced to numbers by algebraic analysis, in which numbers in general are designated by letters. There exists, however, a *higher geometrical analysis* using its own characteristic symbols, which operates much more elegantly and compendiously; specimens are in my possession.

That demonstrations also exist outside the field of magnitude may be evidenced by *formal logic*. Moreover, even the jurists have presented, in the Digests, some truly demonstrated propositions, and I have proposed some specimens in my dissertation *On Conditions*. Johann Suisset, surnamed the Calculator, and others after him, have offered demonstrations in *Metaphysics* concerning the degrees and intensity of the forms. The Platonists and the Aristotelians have said certain things which could without difficulty be rendered in demonstrative form. If we had some exact *language* (like the one called *Adamitic* by some) or at least a kind of *truly philosophic writing*, in which the ideas were reduced to a kind of *alphabet of human thought*, then all that follows rationally from what is given could be found by a *kind of calculus*, just as arithmetical or geometrical problems are solved.

Such a language would amount to a *Cabala* of mystical vocables or to the *arithmetic* of Pythagorean numbers or to the *Characteristic* language of magi, that is, of the wise.

I suspected something of such a great discovery when I was still a boy, and I inserted a description of it in the little book on the *Combinatory Art* which I published in my adolescence.

I can demonstrate with geometrical rigor that such a language is possible, indeed that its foundation can be easily laid within a few years by a number of cooperating scholars.

The study of mathematical analysis provided me with the most genuine and elegant compendium of this *general analysis of human ideas*. I pursued this study so intensely that I doubt whether many contemporaries have invested more work in the same pursuit.

Those who thoroughly delight in such studies will agree that I was the first to clarify certain recondite mathematical problems to the satisfaction of the most eminent mathematicians.

For the Euclidian *axioms and theorems* concerning magnitudes and proportions I substituted others of much greater importance and more general use, concerning *coincidence, congruence, similitude, determinants, cause* and *effect*, i.e., *power, relations in general, containing* and *content*, spontaneous and accidental events, the general nature of substance, the perfect *spontaneity* of substances and the *impossibility of their generation and destruction*, and concerning the *union of all things* and the mutual harmony of all substances. Based on these considerations, I also was able to elucidate the mystery of the *union of soul and body*, the way substances operate, the *concurrence*

of God, the reconciliation of the cause of evil with human freedom and with providence, and the certainty and determinate
truth of contingents. I also substituted *metamorphosis* for
metempsychosis.

In my demonstrations I use *two principles*. The first is this:
What implies contradiction is false. The other is: Reasons can
be given for any truth (which is not immediate or identical);
that is, the predicate concept always inheres in its subject concept, either explicitly or implicitly. This holds true equally in
extrinsic and in intrinsic denominations, in contingent and in
necessary truths.

The difference between *necessary* and *contingent truths* is
indeed the same as that between commensurable and incom-
mensurable numbers. For just as commensurable numbers can
be resolved into common factors, so necessary truths can be
demonstrated, that is, reduced to identical propositions. Moreover: in surd (irrational) ratios the resolution proceeds *in infinitum* and a common measure cannot be attained; yet a certain series is obtained, though it be endless. Analogously, contingent truths require an infinite analysis which can be performed only by God, so that He alone can know them a priori
and with certainty. For although the present state can always
be explained by the preceding, this preceding state can again be
explained, so that the ultimate reason is not reached within the
series. Thus this unending process itself takes the place of a
reason. It could be understood at the very outset that the true
reason for the whole series lies outside of it, in God, the author
of the universe, upon whom earlier and later states equally
depend, more than they depend on each other. Hence, any truth
which is not susceptible of analysis and cannot be demonstrated
by reason, but receives its ultimate reason and certainty from
the divine mind alone, is not a necessary truth. All the truths of
this kind I call *truths of fact*. This is the root of contingency,
and so far as I know, no one has hitherto explained it.

As to the distinction of obscure and clear, confused and distinct, adequate and inadequate, symbolic and intuitive ideas, I

have already explained this in a paper published in the *Acta eruditorum* of Leipzig.[1]

To come back to the representations of ideas by characters: I think that controversies will never end nor silence be imposed upon the *sects*, unless complicated reasonings can be reduced to simple *calculations*, and words of vague and uncertain meaning to determinate *characters*.

What must be achieved is in fact this: that every paralogism be recognized as an *error of calculation*, and that every *sophism*, when expressed in this new kind of notation, appear as a *solecism* or *barbarism*, to be corrected easily by the laws of this philosophical grammar.

Once this is done, then when a controversy arises, disputation will no more be needed between two philosophers than between two computers. It will suffice that, pen in hand, they sit down to their abacus and (calling in a friend, if they so wish) say to each other: *let us calculate.*

To avoid the charge of boasting of, or hoping for, impossible achievements, I must point out that this method (with sufficient study) can still obtain only such results as can be drawn from what is given, however great the skill applied. It can discover everything that is determined by the data, just as is the case with geometrical problems. It is evident that for mere factual truths and for what depends on chance or accident this art of inventing is not competent.

Even after this restriction, some may believe that this art will be of very little use in any matters which require conjecture, such as in research in political or natural history, in the art of assessing products of nature or persons, hence, in community life, medicine, law, military matters, and the government of the state. To this I reply: as far as reason is competent in these matters (and it is highly competent), so far goes the competence of this art, if not much further. For this art is nothing but the supreme elevation of reason and, through the introduction of

---

1 *Reflections on Knowledge, Truth, and Ideas,* this volume, pp. 3–10.

symbols and signs, the *most compendious use* to which human reason can be put.

Therefore, we shall be able to reach a conclusion with the help of this analysis, when without it the result has not been determined by the data or cannot be expressed. In such cases we shall either attain an *infinite approximation* or, when conjectures have to be made, we shall determine by demonstrative reason the *degree of probability* which can be drawn from the data. We shall also know how the given circumstances must be represented by ratios and be stated like an account of receipts and expenses, so that we can decide in favor of what is most in agreement with reason. Though we may sometimes fail in this procedure—just as happens to masters in the game of dice, in which there is an admixture of reason—we shall nevertheless be acting rationally, and for the most part attain what we wish; it is the same with good gamblers and makers of their own good luck—those who, as a proverb says, are sought out by dice and the like. We judge, moreover, that this procedure is not only more likely to succeed, but also *more secure,* and we shall be prepared, if necessary, to purchase the hope of this success at the price of some risk. Nothing better can be expected from human reason. Therefore I am particularly interested in that part of logic, hitherto hardly touched, which investigates the *estimation of degrees of probability* and the weight of proofs, suppositions, conjectures, and criteria. I am also able to show that, in general calculus no less than in the numerical, *tests* or criteria of truth can be invented, which correspond to casting out nines and other similar proofs; indeed, I have already carried this proof from the common numbers to algebra.

However, there will always remain a difference of intellectual gifts, even after the invention and diffusion of this analysis. Some will always think more rapidly and improvise more promptly than others, just as, even after arithmetic was founded and brought to perfection, so that not much is required for its common usage, some people nevertheless perform the longest operations almost without calculation or writing, by mere mental force. In this respect, too, *experience* will always be master; and once the new art is available, men with practice will be superior to others who are less experienced in it, even though the latter may be of equal intelligence and knowledge. If some- one has frequently calculated in a certain way (e.g., with shill- ings and pence), he will remember the results at which he has often arrived and will perform such computations much more promptly than those who are more experienced in other cur- rencies. So too those who have much experience in a certain matter can often substitute the remembrance of events for the necessity of reasoning, and will thus be better at improvisations. Yet it may be affirmed that, once this true art of general analysis is established and taken up by custom, men who understand it and are experienced in it will under otherwise equal conditions be as far superior to all others as the literate is to the illiterate, the learned to the vulgar, the eminent geometrician to the ap- prentice, and the outstanding algebraist to the common calcu- lator. Provided the required intelligence be applied, anyone could with this reliable method find out everything that can be obtained from the available data, with the use of reason, even by the greatest and most experienced mind. The only dif- ference remaining would be one of promptness, which is more important in action than in meditation and invention. For most frequently, especially when the increase of knowledge is the goal, there is no hurry in arriving at it. Even when action is required, men are often guilty of rashness and are in fact forced to make haste through their prior procrastination. As the prov- erb says, the lazy are always in a hurry. Indeed, those whose duty involves action often postpone meditating on the ultimate principles involved; eventually they are forced to decide with- out deliberations, expecting help from pressure and hurry.

Finally, if the invention of the telescope and the microscope has brought so much light into the sciences of nature, it will certainly be understood how much can be achieved by this *new instrument* (*novum organon*) by which the eye of the mind will be sharpened as much as is in the power of man.

It would be rash, however, to promise the perfection of so

great an art as an immediate result of the first efforts. It will grow with human experience, in proportion as (under the guidance of this art itself) more and more important *data* are brought to light. The Chinese are wont to say that he who knows several thousand characters can write most powerfully, but more recondite matters require the attention of a specialized artisan or a greater master. So it is also in our case: The rate of progress achieved, be it by single men, be it by the whole human race, will be recognized as the major *fruit* of a unique art.

Meanwhile our plan is always *to proceed*, as far as possible, *in a definite order*—which hitherto has hardly been done—to elicit from what is given all the possible consequences and, from the treasures which have already been found, to draw, if God grant his blessings, all the *use and benefit* for health of body and perfection of mind.

XV

All human reasoning uses certain signs or characters. Neither the things themselves nor the ideas of the things can always be distinctly present to the mind, nor is this necessary. For the sake of abridgment, signs are therefore substituted for them. For if the geometrician, whenever he refers in his demonstrations to hyperbolas, spirals, or quadratrices, were always forced to have before his mind the exact definitions and constructions of these curves and again the definitions of the terms used therein, he would be very much delayed in new discoveries. And if the arithmetician should, amidst his calculations, be continually thinking of the value of all the signs and symbols he writes down and of the multitude of units represented, he would never be able to complete long calculations—any more than he could handle as many little stones. Even a lawyer, thinking of claims or exceptions or legal privileges, is often unable to run through all their details and essential requirements mentally, nor is it necessary to do so. As a consequence, names have been assigned to contracts, figures, and various other kinds of things, signs to numbers in arithmetic, to magnitudes in algebra. Thus, whatever has been discovered about those objects through experience or reasoning can also receive a sign, which can thereafter be firmly conjoined with the sign standing for the object. Under the term sign I comprehend words, letters; chemical, astronomical, and Chinese figures; hieroglyphs; musical, cryptographic, arithmetic, algebraic notations; and all other symbols which in our thoughts we use for the signified things. When the signs are written, drawn, or carved, they are called characters. They are the more useful, the more they express the concept of the signified thing, so that they can serve not only for representation, but also for reasoning. The signs used in chemistry and astronomy are of no avail in this respect, unless one hopes with John Dee of London, the author of the Hieroglyphical Monad, to uncover in them I know not what mysteries. Nor do I believe that the figures of the Chinese and Egyptians can be of much value for the discovery of truths. The Adamitic language, and certainly its power, are definitely unknown to us, although some writers assert that they know it and can intuit the essences of things in the names given to them by Adam. The natural languages are of very great value in reasoning, but full of innumerable equivocations and unable to function in a calculus: for if they were able to do this, errors in reasoning could be uncovered from the very form and construction of the words, namely, as solecisms and barbarisms. Hitherto only the arithmetical and the algebraic notations have offered this admirable advantage. For in these fields all reasoning consists in the use of characters, and a mental error and an error of calculation are identical.

Having pondered this matter more deeply, it became clear to me long ago that all human ideas (*cogitationes*) can be resolved into a few as their primitives (*primitivas*).[2] If characters were assigned to these primitives, characters for derivative notions could be formed therefrom, and from these it would always be possible to discover the primitive notions (*notiones primitivae*)

2 Compare *Reflections on Knowledge, Truth, and Ideas*, p. 4. See also note 3, p. 20.

which are necessary ingredients; in short, it would be possible to find correct definitions and values and, hence, also the properties which are demonstrably implied in the definitions. Once this is achieved, anyone who in his reasoning and writing is using characters of this kind, will either never fall into error or, if he does, he will always discover his errors himself by the simplest examinations, as anybody else will; and, moreover, he will find the truth which is implied in the available data. If these data should not be sufficient to find what he is searching for, he would see which experiments and notions would still be required, to approach truth as closely as the data permit, either through approximation or through determining the degree of greater probability. Sophisms and paralogisms would here be nothing other than what errors of calculation are in arithmetic and solecisms or barbarisms in speech.

This characteristic art, of which I conceived the idea, would contain the true organon of a general science of everything that is subject matter for human reasoning, but would be endowed throughout with the demonstrations of an evident calculus. It will therefore be necessary to present our characteristic art itself, that is, the art of using signs in a kind of rigorous calculus, as generally as possible. Since no definite result has yet been reached as to the way these signs must be formed, we shall meanwhile follow the example of mathematics for their future formation, and use the letters of the alphabet, or any other arbitrary notation which in the course of our progress will suggest itself as most convenient. Thus, too, the order of the sciences to be treated with the characteristic method will become clear; and it will be evident that elementary arithmetic precedes, and is simpler than, the elements of the logical calculus dealing with the figures and modes of reasoning.

Let there be any *character A* or *B*, or some other notation.

Let the combination of several characters be called a *formula*.

If a given formula be equivalent to a character, so that they can be mutually substituted for each other, let the formula be called the *value* of the character.

The value of a primordial (*primigenius*) character,[3] that is, the value arbitrarily assigned to it and needing no proof, is its *signification*.

Let the relation between those signs which can be substituted for each other according to the laws of the calculus be called *equipollence*.

As will become evident, there are, in addition to equipollence, many other relations, e.g., inclusion, similitude, determination, which will be treated in their places. Thus, relations are to characters and formulas as propositions are to notions, or as the second operation of the mind is to the first.

A *calculus* or *operation* consists in the production of relations, performed through the conversions (*transmutations*) of formulas according to certain prescribed laws. The greater the number of laws or conditions prescribed for a calculation, the more complex is the calculus and the less simple also that characteristic. Hence it appears that formulas (the characters themselves may be considered as the simplest formulas), relations, and operations are like notions, propositions, and syllogisms. There are also *compound relations*, which presuppose certain operations.

Let a character be said to *enter* a formula if it expressly figures there; this character also figures expressly in the signification of the formula. It is said to be *involved* in the formula, if the substitution of equipollents is necessary to bring the sign into the formula.

Characters enter a formula either *absolutely*, i.e., simply, or with a certain *modification*, i.e., in relation to another character. If there is, for instance, a formula $A . (B) . C$, A and C enter it directly, but B obliquely, under A. It may also happen that all the characters enter a formula with a modification. Suppose a formula $\overline{A . B . C} . \overline{L . M . N}$ where $A . B . C$, while they concur in a certain way, at the same time constitute the direct character composed by their fusion, and $L . M . N$ do

---

[3] Leibniz seems here to be speaking of "primitives" in the sense in which he has used the term above and on p. 4. Nonetheless, he does use a different Latin term, indicating that he had a "sufficient reason" for so doing. We have therefore followed this distinction in the translation.

likewise. A character is called *direct*, if it is posited absolutely and expressed otherwise than by the modified characters. The modified character is then called *oblique*. Some characters enter a formula in such a way that they are indistinguishable from one another; other characters enter it separately. A *set* or aggregate is a uniform compound, that is, a formula which can be divided into other formulas only arbitrarily, e.g., A . B, or A . B . C. All composition is either *equiform* or *disquiform*. Examples of equiformity are A . B or $\overline{A . B} . \overline{C . D}$, or $\overline{A . B}$. $\overline{C . D} . \overline{E . F}$, where those characters which are connected by the same *vinculum* always enter the vinculum uniformly. In the relevant case, A and B must be connected by their vinculum in the same way as C and D by theirs, and as A and B, in the same way also $\overline{A . B}$ and $\overline{C . D}$. If two characters enter a vinculum disquiformly, e.g., $\overline{A \vdash B}$, and the one of them, A, with the *following* C which enters the formula, enters uniformly in a new vinculum, e.g., $\overline{\overline{A \vdash B} \, C}$, A will be direct, B oblique. The ultimate direct character is that which terminates the formula. In the formula $L \vdash \overline{A \vdash \overline{BC}} M$, e.g., L and M are the ultimate direct characters, A and B the intermediate. Sometimes characters are uniformly conjoined among themselves, but in such a relationship that the one of them can be taken arbitrarily for absolute, the rest for modified. Something of this kind happens in multiplication: take the formula ab, and let 2 be the value of a and 3 the value of b. You may then understand ab as $2b$, that is, b as absolute and a as the number by which b is multiplied. The contrary, however, is just as feasible, namely: a may be taken for absolute and 3 as its modification, so that a can be understood as tripled in this formula.

Part of a formula may or may not itself be a formula and stand for itself.

CRITICAL REMARKS CONCERNING THE GENERAL PART OF DESCARTES' PRINCIPLES[1]

On the First Part

First Part: On the Principles of Human Knowledge

1. *In the search after truth, one must, once in a lifetime and as far as possible, doubt everything.*

On Article 1. What Descartes says here on the necessity of doubting anything in which there is the slightest uncertainty would have been better expressed by the following more satisfactory and precise principle: The degree of assent or dissent which any proposition deserves must be considered; or still more simply, for every proposition the reasons must be examined. Then the cavilling about the Cartesian doubt would have ceased. But perhaps the author preferred to propose paradoxes, to stimulate the sluggish reader by novelty. I wish, however, that he had himself remembered his precept, or rather that he had realized its true import. We may best explain its sense and use by a geometrical example. It is known that the geometricians have established axioms and postulates on the truth of which all the rest depends. We admit them, on the one hand because they are immediately evident to the mind, and on the other hand because they are confirmed by innumerable experiences. Yet it would be an improvement of science if they were demonstrated. This has indeed been tried with regard to cer-

---

[1] To facilitate the study of this text, we have inserted summaries of all the Articles in Descartes' *Principles* that Leibniz here discusses, each preceding Leibniz' comment on it. These summaries are Descartes' own, from the "Index of Articles" that he himself added to his *Principles*. (See Adam-Tannery, VIII.)

tain axioms, long ago by Apollonius and Proclus, and recently by Roberval.[2] Certainly Euclid himself wished to demonstrate that in any triangle the sum of two sides is greater than the third (which, according to the joke of some ancient author, is known even to asses, which run to their stables in a straight line and not by detours), because he wanted geometrical truth to be based on reasons and not on sensible images. Similarly he might have demonstrated that two straight lines which, if continued, do not coincide, have but one point in common, had he only had a correct definition of the straight line. I am convinced that the demonstration of axioms is extremely useful for the true analysis or art of invention. Therefore, if Descartes had wished to carry out what is best in his precept, he would have had to apply himself to the demonstration of the principles of the sciences and to perform in philosophy what Proclus wished to do in geometry, where it is less necessary. But sometimes our author seems to care more for applause than for certainty. I would not blame him for having sometimes contented himself with verisimilitude, had he not by his professed rigor aroused the mind. Yet I more lightly blame Euclid, who did adopt certain propositions without demonstration, for he has given us the certainty that having admitted a few hypotheses, we may accept all the rest with security and with the same degree of confidence. If Descartes or other philosophers had achieved something similar, we would not be suffering from doubt. The same remark may be addressed also to the skeptics, who despise the sciences under the pretext that they frequently use undemonstrated principles. I myself believe, on the contrary, that the geometricians are praiseworthy because they have stabilized science, using such undemonstrated principles *quasi* props, and have invented the art of progressing, thus inferring

2 The demonstrations of Proclus are found in his Commentary on the first book of the *Elements* of Euclid, published in 1538. Proclus mentions there the attempts at demonstration undertaken by Apollonius. For Leibniz' comments on Roberval's work, see *Philosophische Schriften*, ed. Gerhardt (7 vols.; Berlin, 1875–1890), I, p. 372 and p. 402; *New Essays*, Book IV, chap. 7, paragraph 1; *Opuscules et fragments inédits*, ed. Couturat (Paris, 1903), p. 539.

from a few principles so many consequences. Indeed, had they wished to postpone the invention of theorems and problems until all the axioms and postulates had been demonstrated, we might have no geometry at all to this day.

2. *That what is doubtful should be considered as false.*

On Article 2. For the rest I see no advantage in considering as false what is doubtful. This would not be to eliminate prejudices, but only to change them. If this were meant only as a fiction, he should not have abused it. It will be seen indeed (in article 8) that when he deals with the distinction of mind and body, his position engenders a paralogism.

4. *Why one can place in doubt the truth of sensible things.*

On Article 4. As regards sensible things, all we can or should desire to know of them is that they are consistent among themselves and with uncontested principles. Thus future events could be to a certain degree predicted from past events. Any truth or reality other than that which affords this should not be demanded; the skeptics should not require anything else nor the dogmatists promise more.

5. *Why one can doubt even of mathematical demonstrations.*

On Article 5. The only doubt of which mathematical demonstrations allow is exactly the same as the fear of error in arithmetical calculations. This risk can be met only by repeating the calculation several times, by letting others check it, or by applying proofs. This weakness of the human mind, which is an effect of the weakness of attention and memory, cannot be completely eliminated. It is in vain that Descartes alludes to it here as though he were to propose a remedy. It would suffice if we could achieve as much in the other sciences as in mathematics. For all reasoning, the Cartesian not excepted, however accurate and solid, will always be exposed to this doubt, at whatever conclusion one may eventually arrive regarding a powerful and deceitful demon or the distinction between dream and waking.

6. *That we have free will, hence we are able to refuse our assent to doubtful things, and thus to avoid error.*

On Article 6. We have free will not when we perceive, but when we act. It does not depend on my decision to find honey sweet or bitter, but neither does it depend on my decision whether a proposed theorem appear true or false to me. Consciousness need only examine what appears to it. When we make any statement we always have before our minds either a present sensation or reason, or a present recollection of a past sensation or reason, although in the latter case we are often deceived by faulty recollection or a lapse of attention. But consciousness of what is present or past does not depend upon our decision. We recognize only one function of the will, namely, the power to command attention and intense study; thus, while the will does not produce judgment in us, it can at least exercise an indirect influence on it. Indeed, it often happens that men eventually come to believe what they would like to be true, having accustomed their minds to consider with the greatest attention what they like. By this means they at last satisfy not only the will, but also the conscience. See also article 31.

7. *We are unable to doubt that we exist while we doubt; and this is the first certainty we can get in philosophy.*

On Article 7. Descartes' thesis that the *"I think therefore I am"* is one of the primary truths is excellent. But it would have been only fair not to neglect other truths of the same kind. In general it can be said that all truths are either truths of fact or truths of reason. The first truth of reason is the principle of contradiction, or (which comes to the same) the principle of identity, as Aristotle has correctly pointed out. There are as many primary truths of fact as there are immediate perceptions or, so to speak, consciousnesses. For I am conscious not only of my thinking self, but also of my thoughts, and it is no more true and certain that I think than that I think this or that.

Therefore, one may rightly refer all primary truths of fact to these two: I think, and: Various things are thought by me. From this it follows not only that I am, but also that I am affected in various ways.

8. From this we can also infer the distinction between mind and body, that is, between the thinking and the corporeal thing.

On Article 8. It is not conclusive to argue in the following way: I can assume or imagine that no bodies exist, but I cannot imagine that I do not exist or do not think, consequently I am not a body and thought is not a mode of the body. I am astonished that an eminent man has been able to attribute such consequences to so weak a sophism, but certainly he adds nothing more, at least in this article. His arguments in the *Meditations* will be examined in their place. Those who think that the soul is corporeal will not admit the possibility of maintaining that there are no bodies, but will concede only the possibility of doubting whether bodies do or do not exist, at least so long as the nature of the soul is unknown. And since everybody knows so clearly that his soul exists, he will only acknowledge that it follows from the argument that he can still doubt whether the soul is corporeal. Twist this argument as you will, never will you be able to extort from it anything more. What favors this paralogism is the abuse of the right afforded by article 2 to reject as false what is doubtful. For it is not legitimate to assume that there are no bodies simply because their existence may be doubted; the latter cannot be granted. It would be different if we knew the nature of the soul as perfectly as its existence, for then what does not appear in it could certainly not be attributed to it.

13. In what sense the knowledge of all things depends upon the knowledge of God.

On Article 13. Apropos of article 5, I have already commented on the errors which may arise from the defects of memory and attention, and which may also glide into arithmetical calculations—even when we are in possession of the perfect method, as concerning numbers; and I have pointed out that this warning is useless here, for no method can be devised in which such errors must not be feared, especially when a long series of reasonings is necessary. Therefore, we must have recourse to verification. The reference to God appears here as a sort of theatrical effect. First of all, the strange fiction or doubt—whether we are not made of such stuff that we may err even where there is the greatest evidence—should frighten no one. The very nature of evidence is opposed to it, and the contrary is guaranteed by the experience and the success of our whole lifetime. If this doubt could ever rightfully be raised, it would be forever insuperable for Descartes himself and for anybody else, to whom this objection could always be opposed even if they proposed the most evident things. Furthermore, all this set aside, it must be pointed out that even though the existence of God be denied, this doubt cannot be raised, and if the existence of God be admitted, it is not suppressed. For if only our existence remained possible, even if there were no God, we would not be less capable of grasping the truth; and if the existence of God be admitted, it does not follow therefrom that creatures may not exist which are fallible and imperfect, the more so since it is possible that this imperfection may not be innate but perhaps superadded by a great sin, as the Christian theologians teach concerning original sin. This evil could then not be imputed to God. Although I do not think that God is aptly introduced here, I do believe, but for other reasons, that the true knowledge of God is the principle of superior wisdom. For God is the first cause of all things no less than their ultimate reason; and a thing cannot be known better than by its causes and reasons.

14. *The existence of God can be correctly demonstrated from our concept of God, which implies his necessary existence.*

On Article 14. The demonstration of the existence of God derived from the concept of God seems to have been first invented and proposed by Archbishop Anselm of Canterbury in his book, *Contra Insipientem*,[3] which is preserved. It has been criticized several times by the Scholastic theologians and by the Aquinate himself,[4] from whom Descartes, who knew him very well, seems to have borrowed it. This argument is not without a certain beauty; yet it is imperfect. It runs as follows. Whatever can be demonstrated by inference from the concept of a thing, can be attributed to that thing. Now, from the concept of the most perfect or greatest Being its existence can be inferred. *Ergo*, existence can be attributed to the most perfect Being (God) or, God exists. The minor of the syllogism is demonstrated as follows. The most perfect or greatest being contains all perfections, therefore also existence, which undoubtedly belongs among the perfections, since to exist is more and greater than not to exist. So far the argument. But without introducing perfection or magnitude, one can form an argument which would be even more rigorous and strict, in the following way: The necessary being exists (or, the Being to whose essence existence belongs, or again, the being *a se*, exists), as is manifest by the terms themselves. Now, God is such a Being, by definition, therefore God exists. These arguments are valid, provided it is taken for granted that the most perfect Being or the necessary Being is possible and does not imply contradiction, or, which comes to the same, that an essence from which existence would follow is possible. But so long as that possibility has not been demonstrated, the existence of God cannot be admitted as perfectly demonstrated by such an argument. In general, as I have once pointed out, it should be remembered that from a definition nothing can be inferred with certainty concerning the defined thing unless it is established that what is thus defined is possible. For if it happens to imply a hidden contradiction, some absurdity may be deduced from it. Nevertheless, this argument reveals the exalted privilege of the divine nature, that He need only to be possible in order to exist, while for all other

---

3 St. Anselm, *Liber apologeticus contra Gaunilonem respondentem pro insipiente* (Reply to Gaunilon's "Apology for the Fool"), in Migne, *Patrologiae latinae*, CLVIII, 247.

4 St. Thomas Aquinas, *Summa contra Gentiles* I. 10.

things possibility is insufficient to prove existence. To demonstrate geometrically the existence of God, it remains only, therefore, to demonstrate the possibility of God accurately and with geometrical rigor. Meanwhile, this argument does inspire great confidence in the existence of a thing which in order to exist requires only to be possible. It may be added that there must be a necessary Being because contingent things doubtless do exist.

18. *Other demonstrations of the existence of God.*

On Article 18. The second argument of Descartes—that we have the idea of the most perfect Being and that, consequently, the cause of this idea, that is, the most perfect Being, exists— this argument is still more doubtful than that based on the possibility of God. It, too, has been rejected by many of those who assert with great zeal the possibility and the existence of God. Nor is it correct, as I remember having read somewhere in Descartes, that we have the idea of a thing when we talk of it and understand what we are saying.[5] For it happens frequently that we combine inconsistent notions; when, for instance, we think of the greatest velocity of movement, which undoubtedly is impossible. For then we certainly have no idea, and yet it is certainly possible for us to speak of it, knowing what we are saying. As I have explained elsewhere, the reason is that we often think only confusedly of the object of our thought and that what we are conscious of is not an idea present in our mind, unless we understand of what we are talking and analyze the idea as far as possible.

20. *That we are not the cause of ourselves but are created by God, who therefore must exist.*

On Article 20. The third argument presents, among others, the same defect. For it assumes that we possess the idea of God's

---

[5] See note 2, p. 5. The Cartesians made use of this passage to elicit from it the definition of idea. See, for example, the *Port-Royal Logic*, Part I, chap. 1; Louis de la Forge, *Traité de l'esprit de l'homme* (*Treatise on the Spirit of Man*), chap. 10; Spinoza, *The Cartesian Principles*, Part I, Definition II.

supreme perfection and therefrom concludes that God exists, because we, who have the idea, exist.

21. *That the continuation of our existence suffices to prove the existence of God.*

On Article 21. From our existence at the present moment it follows that we will also exist later, if no reason for change intervenes. Nothing could, therefore, be proved as to the existence of God from the continuation of our existence, unless it were established beforehand that we could not even exist without the effect of divine goodness. For Descartes' reasoning presupposes that every moment of our duration is completely independent of every other, which cannot be conceded.

26. *That we should never try to understand the infinite, but only think that those things the limits of which are unknown are indefinite in extension; for instance, the extension of the world, the divisibility of material particles, the number of stars, etc.*

On Article 26. Though we are finite we yet can know many things about the infinite; for instance, about asymptotes, that is, lines which even extended to infinity continually approach each other but never meet; about surfaces of infinite longitude, the area of which never exceeds that of a given finite area; or about the sums of infinite series. Otherwise we could not know with certainty anything about God. For there is a difference between knowing something about a thing and comprehending it, that is, holding in one's possession whatever is hidden in it.

28. *That we must not investigate final causes but only the efficient causes of created things.*

On Article 28. As regards the ends which God proposed to himself, I am convinced that we can know them and that it is of the greatest usefulness to investigate them. Whoever despises such an investigation exposes himself to danger and suspicion. In general, whenever we realize that a certain thing renders some eminent services we can safely affirm that this, among others, was the end intended by God when he created that thing, namely, that it should render this service; for he has foreseen and produced this utility of the thing. I have elsewhere shown and confirmed by examples that the consideration of final causes may lead to the discovery of some concealed and very important truths in the natural sciences, the discovery of which would not have been equally easy by the consideration of efficient causes.[6]

30. *Therefrom it follows that all that we clearly perceive is true, which delivers us from the doubts proposed above.*

On Article 30. Even if we admit that the perfect substance exists and is by no means the cause of imperfections, we do not thereby get rid of those true or fictitious reasons of doubt which Descartes has introduced. This I have already pointed out apropos of article 13.

31. *That our errors, when referred to God, are only negations; if referred to ourselves, privation.* —32. *That there are in us only two kinds of thoughts, perceptions of the intellect and operations of the will.* —33. *That we fall into error when we judge about a thing not sufficiently known.* —34. *That the will is required for judgment no less than the understanding.* —35. *That the will has a wider scope than the understanding and that this is the cause of our errors.*

On Articles 31 to 35. I do not agree that our errors depend upon our will rather than on our understanding. To believe what is true or what is false—that is to say, to know or to err—is nothing else than the consciousness or remembrance of perceptions or reasons, and therefore does not depend on our will. It

6 *Unicum opticae, catoptricae et dioptricae principium (A Single Principle of Optics, Catoptrics, and Dioptrics),* 1682 (*Opera*, ed. Dutens [6 vols.; Geneva, 1768—], III, 145). Compare *Discourse on Metaphysics,* paragraphs 21 and 22; *New Essays,* Book IV, chap. 7.

would depend on our will only when and insofar as we eventually, by some unfair means, persuade ourselves of the truth (which we may not know) of what we want to be true. See also what has been said apropos of article 6. We judge, therefore, according to what presents itself to our consciousness, and not according to our will. As to Descartes' opinion that the will has a wider scope than the understanding, it is more shrewd than true; this is catering to the popular taste. Our will aims only at what is presented to the understanding. The origin of all errors is the same in a certain sense as that of the errors of calculation which occur in arithmetic. For it frequently happens that, due to deficient memory or attention, we do what ought not to be done or omit what ought to be done, or we believe that we have already done what we have not done or that we have not done what actually we have done. Thus it happens in calculations (to which reasoning corresponds in the mind) that one forgets to introduce certain necessary signs while introducing certain others which are out of place; or that one neglects some element of the calculation in the process of summing up; or that one operates against the rules of method. When our mind is tired or distraught it does not pay sufficient attention to the operations which it is about to perform or, due to an error of memory, it accepts as already proved what is only deeply rooted in us as the effect of frequent repetition or of long examination or of an ardent wish. The remedy for our errors is also the same as that for errors of calculation: to focus the attention on matter as well as on form, to proceed slowly, to repeat and vary the operation, to apply verifications and proofs, to cut very long chains of reasoning into parts, so that the mind gets a breathing spell, and to get confirmation of each part by special proofs. And since action sometimes requires promptness, it is important to acquire the habit of presence of mind like those persons who are able, even in the midst of noise and without written calculation, to perform operations on very high numbers. The mind thus accustoms itself to resist distraction either by external sensations or by its own imaginations and emotions, and to rise above its doings, to keep its power of reflecting on itself, or, as it is commonly called, of self-criticism. Thus it will become able to warn itself continually like a monitor from outside: Look what you are doing! Why are you doing it? Time flies! The Germans, very appropriately, call this *sich begreiffen*, the French, no less well, *s'aviser*, as if one advised oneself or made suggestions to oneself. The mind acts then like the Roman *nomenclators* who supplied candidates with the names and titles of the citizens whose votes were worthy of solicitation, or like the prompter who whispers to the actors the first words of the line to come, or like the youth who repeated to King Philip of Macedonia the famous words: Forget not, thou art mortal! But it is not in our power, nor does it depend upon our will, to reflect on ourselves, *s'aviser*. This attitude must first occur to the intellect and depends upon our present degree of perfection. It is up to the will to strive beforehand with all possible zeal to prepare the mind well for this discipline; this preparation may be achieved usefully both by the study of the experiences, dangers, or damages encountered by others, and by learning from our own experiences, I mean from those which were, as far as possible, exempt from danger or accompanied by only slight and negligible inconvenience. The same result can be achieved by training the mind to think in good methodical order, so that afterward what is required offers itself spontaneously to consciousness. It may nevertheless happen, without our fault, that things escape us or do not offer themselves promptly. In this case it is not a defect of judgment which is to be blamed, but a shortcoming of our memory or our natural intellectual capacities, and in these cases we do not fall into error, but are simply ignorant. But this does not belong to our subject matter, since it is not in our power to know or to remember everything we wish. It is sufficient to become accustomed to that kind of critical reflection by which we can fight against the lack of attention. It is also sufficient that, whenever our memory makes us believe that proofs have already been given, while actually this perhaps has not been the case, we hold this confused recollection suspect, and either repeat the research, if the issue is important, or trust only those recollections which report past efforts with sufficient evidence.

37. Man's greatest perfection is the power of free will, and this is what renders him worthy of praise or blame.

On Article 37. Man's greatest perfection is to act reasonably no less than to act freely; or rather, the two are one and the same, since he is the more free the less the use of his reason is troubled by the influence of passion.

39. That our free will is known without proof, solely by our experience of it.

On Article 39. To ask whether freedom depends upon our will is the same as to ask whether our will depends upon our will. For free and voluntary mean the same.[7] Freedom is spontaneity directed by reason, and to will is to be carried to action by reasons perceived by the intellect. Action is free in proportion as reason is pure and unclouded by brute and confused perceptions. It does not depend upon our will to abstain from judging; this is the business of the understanding, imposing upon itself critical reflection, as has been said apropos of article 35.

40. It is certain that all things have been preordained by God. —41. How our free will and the divine preordination can be reconciled.

On Article 40. Some people may be convinced that God has preordained all things and that none the less they are free, and may be satisfied with replying to those who show that the two assertions are incompatible, what Descartes suggests, namely, that our minds are finite and unable to understand such things.

---

[7] Compare Descartes: "To do a thing *freely*, or to do it *willingly*, or to do it *voluntarily*, are one and the same thing." (Letter to Mersenne, Adam-Tannery, III, 381.)

This seems to amount to answering the conclusion but not the reasons and to cutting the knot without solving it. The question is not whether the matter itself is understood, but rather whether, once I have shown you the inconsistency of the argument, you understand your own absurdity. For even the mysteries of faith must be noncontradictory; so much more so the mysteries of nature. Hence, if you want to think philosophically, it will be necessary that you take up again any reasoning which has some apparent justification and yet seems to involve contradiction and that you find out where the mistake lies. This certainly can always be done, unless the whole argument is erroneous.

43. *That we never fall into error if we accept only what we perceive clearly and distinctly.* —44. *That we always judge wrongly when we accept what is not clearly perceived, even though we may by chance hit upon the truth; such errors happen because we suppose that we have previously had a sufficiently clear perception.* —45. *What perceptions are clear and what distinct.* —46. *It is shown by the example of pain that a perception can be clear without being distinct, but not distinct without being clear.*

On Articles 43 to 46. Elsewhere[8] I have commented on the scanty usefulness of that much praised rule: Only what is clear and distinct ought to be accepted as true. It has no value unless better criteria of clearness and distinctness than those given by Descartes are established. The rules of Aristotle and of the geometricians are still preferable, enjoining one to admit nothing (except primary truths and hypotheses) which has not been demonstrated by a correct argument—correct, in that it does not suffer from a formal or material vice. A material vice consists in accepting as true anything except the principles or what in its turn has been deduced from them by a correct demonstration. By a correct form I understand not only the common syllogism, but any other form which has been demonstrated beforehand and concludes through the form of its structure. This is the case

8 *Reflections on Knowledge, Truth, and Ideas,* this volume, pp. 3–10.

with the forms of the arithmetical and algebraic operations, the forms of accounting books, and in a certain sense the forms of judicial procedure. For sometimes we are satisfied in practical life with a certain degree of verisimilitude. It is true that the part of logic so very useful in life, which deals with the estimation of degrees of probability, remains to be investigated. I have myself studied quite a few parts of this science. On form see also below, on article 75.

47. *That to eliminate the prejudices of our childhood, the simple notions have to be studied; on what is clear in each of them.* —48. *That everything which is an object of our perception can be considered either as a thing or as the affection of a thing or as an eternal truth; enumeration of the things.*

On Articles 47, 48. Someone (I don't know who it was, but I think it was Comenius) has once remarked that Descartes, after having promised in article 47 to enumerate summarily all simple notions, abandons us immediately in article 48, and after having named some of them continues: *and others of the kind.* Incidentally, most of those he names are not simple. Yet this question is more important than is generally realized.

50. *Eternal truths are clearly perceived, but not all of them by everyone, because of prejudices.*

On Article 50. As to relatively simple truths which men's prejudiced opinions yet prevent them from adopting, it is advisable to demonstrate them by still simpler ones.

51. *Definition of substance and that this name is not applied in the same sense to God and to creatures.*

On Article 51. If you define substance as that which needs only divine support in order to exist, I do not know whether this covers any created substance known to us, unless you interpret the definition in an unusual way. For to exist we need not only other substances, but still more our own accidents. Hence substance and accident being mutually interdependent, we will need other criteria to distinguish a substance from an accident. Such a criterion could be, for instance, that substance needs some accident but often not one individually determined accident, so that if a definite accident is removed, the lack is satisfied by the substitution of another. On the other hand, in general, an accident needs not only a substance, but that substance in which it is inherent, so that it cannot change its substance. There remain to be investigated, however, other profound and important problems on the nature of substance.

52. *That the notion of substance applies equally to the mind and to the body, and how we know substance.*

On Article 52. I agree that each substance has a principal attribute which expresses its essence. But I doubt whether in the case of individual substances this essence can be explained in a few words as it is possible to do in the case of generic substances which can be explained by their definitions. That extension is the common nature of the corporeal substance is a doctrine taught with great confidence by many, but never proved. Certainly neither motion, that is, action, nor resistance or passive force, can be derived therefrom. Nor can the laws of nature concerning the motion and the shock of bodies be derived from the concept of extension, as I have shown elsewhere. As a matter of fact, the notion of extension is not primitive but can be resolved. For the extended thing must be a continuous whole in which several parts exist simultaneously. Furthermore, extension, the notion of which is relative, requires something which extends or is continued, as in milk, whiteness, and in bodies, that which constitutes their essence; whatever this may be, its repetition is extension. I completely agree with Huygens—of whose achievements in natural science and mathematics I have a high opinion—that the concepts of empty space and extension are identical. And to my mind mobility or ἀντιτυπία[9] cannot

___

[9] *Antitupia,* a term of Stoic physics that designates the resistance or impenetrability of bodies.

be understood by extension alone, but requires a subject which extends and which does not only constitute the place, but fills it.

54. How we can have clear and distinct notions of the thinking substance, the corporeal substance, and even God.

On Article 54. I do not remember that Descartes or his followers have ever perfectly demonstrated that the thinking substance lacks extension, or the extended substance, thought. This demonstration would be necessary to establish that the two attributes do not require each other in the same subject, that they are indeed incompatible in it. This is not astonishing, for the author of *The Search After Truth* (who has called attention to many very important things) has correctly remarked that the Cartesians have not proposed any distinct concept of thought, so that obviously they have not realized what this concept implies.[10]

60. On distinctions, and first on real distinctions. —61. On modal distinctions.

On Articles 60, 61. To deny the real distinction of modes is to change without necessity the traditional usage of words. For up to now modes have also been counted among things and it has been thought that they really are distinct, as for instance, the spherical and the cubic shape of a piece of wax. The transformation of one shape into the other is certainly a true change, hence has a real foundation.

63. How we can have distinct ideas of thought and extension as constituting, the one, the nature of the soul, and the other, the nature of the body.

On Article 63. It is neither correct nor possible, I think, to conceive thought or extension as being themselves the thinking

[10] Malebranche, *Recherche de la Vérité* (*The Search After Truth*), Book III, Part II, chap. 7, paragraph 4, and Clarification XI.

or the extended substance. This crafty scheme is suspect and resembles the one enjoining that doubtful things be considered false. By such distortions minds become prepared to obstinacy and paralogisms.

65. *How the modes of mind and body can be known.* —66. *How the senses, passions, and appetites can be clearly known, though our judgment about them is often wrong.* —67. *That we are often deceived in our judgment about pain.* —68. *That we must distinguish in these things that which is clearly known from that in which we may be deceived.*

On Articles 65 to 68. Following the ancients, Descartes has rendered us good service in eradicating the prejudice that heat, color, and other phenomena are considered as things outside ourselves. It is known, indeed, that what a moment ago has been felt as hot may shortly afterward be felt as tepid by the same hand; that he who sees a mixed powder as green will no longer see this color when he uses a magnifying glass, but will perceive a mixture of yellow and blue powder; with a more powerful glass or with the help of other experiments or reasonings, he may even be able to discover the causes of the two latter colors. Whence it is evident that outside of us nothing exists which would resemble the image appearing to our imagination. In this respect we are like children who believe that at the end of the rainbow where it touches the earth there is a pot of gold, which they run after in vain.

71. *That the first and principal cause of our errors arises from the prejudices of our childhood.* —72. *The second is that we are unable to forget those prejudices.* —73. *The third cause is that our attention easily tires when we consider things that are not present to the senses, and that therefore we are wont to judge about them not according to the present perception, but according to preconceived ideas.* —74. *The fourth cause is that we associate our concepts with words which do not exactly correspond to the concepts.*

On Articles 71 to 74. We have already made some remarks on the cause of error apropos of articles 31 and 35. From what has been said there, the errors mentioned in articles 71 to 74 can also be explained. For the prejudices of childhood also belong to the unproved assumptions, fatigue diminishes attention, and the ambiguity of words is a special case of the bad use of signs and constitutes a vice of form. It is the same error as that which, according to a German proverb, consists in putting in a calculation an 'x' for a 'u,' or as that which the pharmacist commits when in a prescription he reads *sandaraca* for *sanguis draconis.*

75. Brief summary of the rules of correct philosophical thought.

On Article 75. It would be fair, I think, to attribute to the ancients what is due to them and not to obfuscate their merits by a silence which is spiteful and harmful to ourselves. What Aristotle has taught in his Logic may not be sufficient to discover truth, yet it usually suffices to judge correctly where we only deal with necessary consequences. It is very important, indeed, that the consequences inferred by the human mind be guaranteed by certain rules analogous to the rules of mathematical operations. I have observed that those who in serious reasoning fall into paralogisms sin more frequently than is generally admitted against the formal rules of logic. To avoid all errors nothing more is required, therefore, than to use the most common rules of logic with great constancy and rigor. But frequently the complication of matters does not allow such meticulousness. That is why in the sciences and in practice we apply special logical forms which have to be demonstrated beforehand on the basis of those general rules and adapted to the particular nature of the subject matter. Euclid proceeded in this manner; he has his own logic for the conversion, composition, and division of ratios, a logic which he first proves in a special book of his *Elements*[11] and afterward observes in his whole geometry. By this means one promotes at the same time economy and security

[11] It is Book V.

of thought; and the more methods of this kind science possesses the more will it advance. One may add here what I have said apropos of articles 43 ff. concerning the advantage of using arguments operating by virtue of form much more widely than is usually thought possible.

On the Second Part

Second Part: On the Principles of Material Things

1. *What reasons make us know with certainty that material things exist.*

On Article 1. The argument by which Descartes tries to demonstrate the existence of material things is very weak indeed; it would have been better had he not tried. The core of his argument is this: The reason for our sensation of material things is outside of us; therefore, these sensations come to us either from God, or from some other agent, or from the things themselves. They do not come from God, if these things do not exist; for otherwise God would be a deceiver; they do not come from another agent—this he forgot to prove; therefore they come from the things themselves, which therefore must exist. It may be answered that the sensations may come from an agent other than God; for just as, for some weighty reasons, he permits other evils, he may also permit this deceit, without thereby becoming a deceiver; the more so since this deception does not entail any damage to us and since, in this respect, it would be rather to our disadvantage not to be deceived. There is, besides, a sophism in this argument: Descartes conceals in it the possibility that our sensations may come from God or some other agent, while the judgment on their cause—namely whether they are produced by real external objects—and hence the deception, may be imputed to ourselves. We deceive ourselves indeed when we take colors and other sensations of this sort for real objects. Moreover, our souls may have deserved because of former sins to be condemned to this life full of deceptions, in which they take shadows for things. The Platonists do not seem to have rejected this theory: life here below appeared to them comparable to a dream in the cave of Morpheus, the mind having lost reason by drinking from the river Lethe before coming to this world, as the poets said in their songs.

4. *That neither weight nor hardness nor color, etc., constitutes the nature of bodies, but extension alone.*

On Article 4. Descartes attempts to demonstrate that bodies consist exclusively in extension, by first enumerating and then eliminating all the other attributes. But he ought to have proved that his enumeration is complete. Moreover, the elimination of the other attributes is not always convincing. Those who defend the theory of atoms, that is, of perfectly hard bodies, deny that hardness consists in their resistance to being moved by our hands, but affirm that it consists in their preserving their figures. And those who think that the essence of bodies consists in ἀντιτυπία [*antitupia*] or impenetrability do not draw their concept of bodies from what our hands or senses teach us, but from the experience that a body does not yield its place to another body unless the first can go elsewhere. If we imagine, for instance, that a cube be struck simultaneously by six other cubes moving with equal velocity and equal in mass to the first and among themselves, so that each one of the six exactly covers with one of its surfaces one surface of the cube receiving the shock, it will be impossible that either the receiving cube or any part of it perform any local movement, whether the cube be elastic or rigid. While if we suppose the cube in the middle to be penetrable extension, that is, mere space, then the six converging cubes may stop each other with their edges; but if they are elastic, there will be no obstacle to the penetration of their middle parts into the space of the receiving cube. One can understand therefrom the difference between hardness, which belongs only to certain bodies, and impenetrability, which belongs to all of them. This impenetrability Descartes ought to have taken into consideration no less than hardness.

5. That the phenomena of rarefaction and condensation obscure this nature of bodies. —6. On rarefaction. —7. That it cannot be explained intelligibly otherwise than here proposed.

On Articles 5 to 7. Here Descartes explains very well that rarefaction and condensation as we perceive them by our senses may well take place without forcing us to admit that matter is interspersed with empty spaces, nor that the same part of matter changes dimensions.

8. That magnitude differs from what has magnitude, and number from what is numbered only in our thought. —9. When corporeal substance is distinguished from its quantity it is confusedly conceived as if it were incorporeal. —10. On space or internal place. —11. That it is not really different from the substance of a body. —12. That the difference lies only in the mode of conception. —13. On external place. —14. On the difference of place and space. —15. That the external place may be rightly identified with the surface of the enveloping bodies. —16. That the existence of a vacuum, that is, of space without anything in it, is inadmissible. —17. That the vacuum as popularly conceived does not exclude all bodies. —18. How one may correct the opinion concerning an absolute vacuum. —19. That this confirms what has been said above on rarefaction.

On Articles 8 to 19. Many of those who admit the vacuum consider space as a substance and cannot be refuted by the arguments of Descartes. To end this controversy different principles are needed. Those philosophers will concede that quantity and number cannot subsist without the things to which they are attributed, but they will deny that space or place is the quantity of bodies. They will rather think that space itself has a certain quantity or capacity equal to that of the body contained in this space. Descartes ought to have shown that space or the internal capacity does not differ from the substance of the body. Those who hold the opposite opinion will base themselves on the notion common to all mortals, namely, that a body succeeding another enters the same place and the same space which this other has left—an opinion which cannot be maintained if space coincides with the very substance of the body. For even though it be an accident of the body to be in a certain place or a given space, it cannot be admitted that place itself is an accident of the body. One might as well argue that because contact is an accident, that which is touched is an accident, too.

Descartes seems to me to be less bent, in this context, on providing his own theses with valid proofs than on refuting the opposite arguments, and this he does quite successfully. It is not rare to see him using this artifice in lieu of demonstrating. Yet we were expecting more than that and, if I am not mistaken, were encouraged to expect more. That nothing has no extension must be acknowledged, and Descartes rightly attacks those who admit some kind of unintelligible imaginary space. But those who consider space as some kind of substance are not affected by this argument; they would be affected, however, if Descartes had previously proved what he merely assumes here, namely that all extended substance is a body.

20. *Hence it follows that there can be no atoms.*

On Article 20. The author does not seem to refute atomism satisfactorily: the atomists may concede that atoms can be divided in thought as well as by divine power. But whether in nature there can exist bodies the hardness of which is insuperable by natural forces—which is the true doctrine of the atomists—this is a question which Descartes, surprisingly, does not even touch upon in this context. Yet he claims here to have destroyed the atoms and takes this for granted in all the rest of his work. I shall add something more about the atoms apropos of article 54.

21. *That the extension of the world is indefinite.* —22. *That matter is the same in the skies and on earth, and that there can-*

not be several worlds. —23. That all the varieties of matter and all the diversities of its forms depend upon motion.

On Articles 21 to 23.   That the extension of the world has no ends and that therefore there can be only one world, that matter is everywhere homogeneous, and therefore differentiated only through figure and motion: these theses are proclaimed here though it is neither generally admitted nor demonstrated by the author that extension and body are the same.

25. What is motion, properly speaking.

On Article 25.   If motion were nothing else but a change of contact or immediate contiguity it would follow that it would be impossible to determine which object is moving; for just as in astronomy one can explain the same phenomena by different hypotheses, so it will always be possible to attribute real motion to one or to another of the bodies which change their relative position or vicinity. Hence, one could arbitrarily consider one or another as being at rest or as moving with a given velocity along a given line, and then determine geometrically what motion or rest has to be attributed to the others so that the given phenomena ensue. It follows therefrom that, if nothing else but this reciprocal change constitutes motion, there is no natural reason why motion should be ascribed to one object rather than to others. Hence there would be no real motion at all. To be able to say that an object is moving, we will require, therefore, not only that it change its position with respect to others, but also that this body contain in itself the cause of change, a force, an action.

26. That no more action is required for motion than for rest.

On Article 26.   From what has been said in the preceding paragraph, it becomes evident that Descartes' affirmation in this article—namely that in bodies motion requires no more action than rest—cannot be maintained. I agree that a body at rest needs force to remain at rest despite the shock of other bodies striking it. But this force does not reside in the body at rest but is the effect of the conflicting forces of the moving bodies which surround it, thus coercing the body at rest to remain in its former position.

32. *How even motion in the proper sense, which is a single motion in any body, may be considered as several.*

On Article 32. The earliest of all authors whose work is extant and who dealt with the composition of motions was Archimedes, in his treatment of spirals. The first who applied this theory to explain the equality of the angles of incidence and reflection was Kepler, in his *Paralipomena optica*,[12] where he decomposes the oblique motion into a perpendicular and a parallel motion. Descartes has followed him here as well as in his *Dioptrics*. But the first to show the wide use of the composition of motions in physics and mechanics was Galileo.

33. *How every motion involves an entire circle of bodies simultaneously moving.* —34. *That hence it follows that matter is divided into indefinitely small particles, though these are incomprehensible for us.* —35. *How this division is produced, and that we must not doubt it, though we are unable to comprehend it.*

On Articles 33 to 35. What Descartes says here is very excellent and worthy of his genius—namely, that every motion in a plenum involves circular motion, and that matter must somewhere be actually divided into parts which are smaller than any given magnitude. But he does not seem to have sufficiently elaborated on this last and very important conclusion.

36. *That God is the primary cause of motion, and that he always conserves the same quantity of motion in the universe.*

[12] Kepler, *Astronomiae pars optica, seu paralipomena in Vitellionis Opticam*, Frankfort, 1604.

On Article 36. That the same quantity of motion is conserved in the universe—this is the most famous theory of the Cartesians. Yet they have given no demonstration of it, for the argument based on God's constancy which is given here, is so weak that it cannot convince anyone. Indeed, even if God's constancy be absolute and he should change nothing except according to the laws of an order established long ago, it must still be asked what it is that God decided to conserve in the series of changes. It might be the quantity of motion, but it might as well be something different from it, for instance, the quantity of force. I have demonstrated that it is, indeed, rather the quantity of force which is preserved, and that this is different from the quantity of motion. I have also demonstrated that it very frequently happens that the latter changes, while the quantity of force is always permanent. One may read elsewhere in greater detail the arguments whereby I proved this and how I vindicated my theory against objections. Since, however, the question is of great importance, I wish summarily to explain the source of my reflections by an example. Suppose two bodies, *A* with mass 4 and velocity 1, and *B* with mass 1 and velocity 0, that is, at rest. Imagine now that the total force of *A* be transmitted to *B*, that is, that *A* be reduced to rest, while *B* alone moves instead; the question then is what velocity *B* will acquire. According to the Cartesians it will be answered: *B* will have the velocity 4, so that the former quantity of motion and the present are equal, because the mass 4 times the velocity 1 is the same as the mass 1 times the velocity 4. Velocity thus will be increased in proportion as mass has been diminished. According to my own theory, it must be answered that *B* (mass 1) will acquire the velocity 2 in order to have the same power which *A* (mass 4) had when moving with the velocity 1. But I must explain the reason for this in brief to avoid the impression that my theory is arbitrary. My contention is that only in this way will *B* have the same power now which *A* had before, or, will the present and the former power be equal; this it is worthwhile to prove. To begin with a more general consideration, I shall explain the true method of estimation, which is the function of a truly universal mathematics, though this science has never been taught before. It is evident, first of all, that the power is doubled, tripled, quadrupled when that which has the simple power is exactly repeated two, three, or four times. Hence two bodies with equal masses and velocities will have double the power of one of them. But it does not follow therefrom that a body having double the velocity of another has only twice its power. For though in the latter case the degree of velocity is once repeated, the subject of movement is not thereby repeated; a mere duplication of power results only when a body is replaced by another of twice its mass or by two bodies equal to the replaced in mass and velocity. Similarly a weight of two pounds lifted to the height of one foot above the horizontal is exactly the double, as to mass and to force, of one pound lifted to the same altitude; and two springs with equal tension are the double of one of them. But take the case of two objects which have the same power but are not homogeneous: then they cannot be compared to each other by this means nor reduced to a common measure of mass and force. In such a case an attempt must be made to compare them in a roundabout way, namely, by comparing either the homogeneous effects produced by them or their causes. For any cause has a power equal to its total effect, that is, to the effect it produces in spending its power.

Now the two bodies in the above example, A with mass 4 and velocity 1, and B with mass 1 and velocity 2, cannot be exactly compared to each other, nor is it possible to measure both of them by a unit of power, the simple repetition of which would produce both. Therefore, we have to examine their effects. Let us suppose, then, that these two bodies are subject to gravitation: if therefore A, changing its direction, ascends and by means of its velocity 1 can rise to the altitude of 1 foot, then B with the velocity 2 will be able to rise to an altitude of 4 feet, as Galileo and others have demonstrated. In either case the effects will be total, consuming the whole power of each body, and therefore equal also to the producing cause. But these two effects are equal to each other as to force or power: the elevation of four pounds (body A) to the altitude of one foot, and the elevation of one pound (body B) to the altitude of four feet. Therefore, also the causes, namely A (mass 4, velocity 1) and B (mass 1, velocity 2), will be equal in force or power, as we have maintained. Should somebody deny, however, that the two effects, the elevation of four pounds one foot high and of one pound four feet high, are equivalent—although as far as I know almost everybody agrees—he can be convinced by reference to the same principle. Let us take scales with unequal arms: if on the one side one pound descends by four feet, on the other side four pounds can be lifted by one foot, and this will be the total effect produced. Here again the effect consumes exactly the power of the cause, which proves that its force equals that of the cause. From this I infer the following: if the total power of A (mass 4, velocity 1) is to be communicated to B (mass 1, at rest), B must acquire the velocity 2; or, which comes to the same: if B has been at rest and A moving, and after the shock A comes to rest and B is to move (all other conditions remaining identical), the velocity of B must be twice that of A before the shock, if the mass of A is four times that of B. If, however, the generally accepted Cartesian theory were correct, B, the subquadruple of A, that is, equal in weight to the fourth part of A, would acquire four times the velocity of A. But then we would have a case either of perpetual motion or of an effect exceeding the power of its cause. For at first, when A was moving, four pounds could be lifted one foot high, or one pound, four feet high; after the shock, when B has been set moving, one pound could be lifted sixteen feet high, for the elevations are proportional to the squares of those velocities by the force of which they can be reached, and the quadruple velocity lifts sixteen times as high. By the force of B we could, therefore, not only lift A one foot high, from which height it would redescend and acquire its prior velocity; we could do much more with it. This would indeed be a case of perpetual mechanical motion, since the original power is restituted and yet an excess remains unspent. Possibly our supposition concerning the transfer of the total power of A to B could not be completely actualized; but this would not change anything, since we are dealing here with the true estimation, that is, with the velocity B must acquire according to our hypothesis. For even though only part of the force is communicated and another part retained, the same absurdities must result; for if the quantity of motion is to be conserved, it is evident that the quantity of force could not always be conserved. Indeed, the quantity of motion obviously is in proportion to mass and velocity, while, as we have shown, the quantity of power is in proportion to the mass and to the height to which a heavy body can be carried by this power. But the heights are proportional to the squares of the velocities of the ascending bodies. At this point one can already establish this rule: The same quantity of force as well as of movement is conserved when the two bodies, both before and after their shock, move in the same direction, and also when the two colliding bodies have the same masses.

37. *The first law of nature: that every thing, insofar as it depends on itself, remains always in the same state, so that once moved it will always continue to move.* —38. *On projectile motion.*

On Articles 37, 38. It is a true and uncontested law of nature that anything, insofar as it depends on itself, always remains in the same state. Galileo, Gassendi, and many others have known it long since. It is so much more astonishing that there are scientists who imagined that the continuation of projectile motion was due to the movement of the air; it evidently did not occur to them that, with the same right, one would have to ask for a new cause of the continuation of the movement of the air itself. For the air could not push on a thrown stone, as those men believed, unless it had in itself the force of continuing the movement once received, and unless this force were hindered by the resistance of the stone.

39. *The second law of nature: that all motion, if continued independently, is rectilinear, and that bodies which move in a circle always tend to move away from the center of the circle which they are describing.*

On Article 39. It is an admirable law of nature that a body moving in a circle or any other curved line tends to depart from its path in a straight tangent. But this law has not only been observed by Kepler (perhaps even before him by others), but— which I admire still more—he had already used it, as appears from his *Epitome astronomiae Copernicanae.*[13] Descartes has correctly formulated this law and very well explained it, but he has not demonstrated it, as one could have expected of him.

40. *The third law: that a body striking against a stronger one loses nothing of its movement; if it strikes a less strong one, it loses as much as it communicates to the other.* —41. *Proof of the first part of this rule.* —42. *Proof of the second part.* —43. *In what consists the force of each body to act or to resist.* —44. *That movement is not contrary to movement but to rest; and the determination in one direction contrary to the determination in the opposite direction.*

On Articles 40 to 44. In articles 37 and 39, Descartes has formulated two very true laws of nature which are almost self-evident. But the third law, proposed here, is, it seems to me, not only so far from truth, but also from probability, that I wonder that such a great mind could have conceived it. And yet this is the foundation on which he soon bases his rules of motion and the shock of bodies, claiming that all the causes of particular changes in bodies are implied in it. He formulates this law as follows: If a body in motion collides with another which has a greater force, the first will lose nothing of its movement but only change its determination; it may, however, acquire some motion from the stronger body. While, colliding with a less strong body, it will lose as much of its movement as it communicates to the less strong body. In truth, however, the law according to which a body colliding with a stronger body loses nothing of its movement but only keeps or increases its velocity is a law valid only when the shock occurs between two bodies moving in opposite directions. But when a less strong but faster

---

13 Kepler, *Epitome astronomiae Copernicanae,* Linz, 1618.

moving body catches up with a body of greater strength but lower velocity running before it, the contrary happens. And in general I find that nature obeys a law according to which the velocity of a body catching up with another running before it is diminished by the shock. For if after the shock it continues its motion, it cannot possibly continue it with its former velocity, without communicating this velocity also to the body it pushes from behind. But in this case the total sum of power would be increased. If it comes to rest after the shock, it is clear *per se* that its velocity has not only been diminished by the shock, but annihilated; for hard bodies (such I always suppose them here) come to a stop when the ratio of the excess of the mass of the preceding body over the body which follows to the preceding body[14] is double the ratio of the velocity of the preceding body to the velocity of the following body. Finally, if the body which follows is reflected after the shock, it is again clear that the motion of the reflected body is smaller than before the shock; otherwise, if we want at any price to have the velocity of the following body after the reflection also increased or at

14 The text of Leibniz reads "when the ratio of the excess of the preceding body over the following to the *following* is double. . . ." It is undoubtedly necessary to correct the reading, as we have done.

Let us designate the mass of the preceding body by m, its velocity before and after the shock by v and v', the mass of the body which overtakes it by m_1, its velocity by v_1 and v_1'. Their relations are determined by these two equations:

$$mv^2 + m_1v_1^2 = mv'^2 + m_1v_1'^2 \quad \text{(conservation of force)}$$
$$mv + m_1v_1 = mv' + m_1v_1' \quad \text{(conservation of motion)}$$

In order for m_1 to be stopped after the shock, that is to say, for $v_1' = 0$, it is necessary that $\dfrac{m - m_1}{m} = \dfrac{2v}{v_1}$.

One can, with the aid of these two fundamental equations, explain without difficulty the entire discussion of the laws of the shock of bodies which follows, observing, however, that according to the second equation, it is the *algebraic* sum of the quantities of motion which is conserved, and not the absolute sum, as Descartes had asserted. The forces in opposite directions ought, then, to appear here with opposite signs. That is the reason why Leibniz, at the end of article 36, restricted the principle of the conservation of the quantity of motion, taken in the Cartesian sense, to cases in which the two bodies, before and after meeting, move in the same direction.

least remaining equal to its velocity before the shock, the total sum of powers would again be increased, which is absurd. For the velocity of the preceding body which received the shock must necessarily be increased by the impact of the shock.

If, to vindicate Descartes, someone should object that this third law on the shock of bodies refers only to the shock of bodies coming from opposite directions, I would agree. But then it would have to be admitted that Descartes has not taken care of the shock of bodies moving in the same direction. And yet he has claimed, as I have already pointed out, that this same law covers all particular cases. The demonstration attempted in article 41, if true, would also cover all the cases of shocks of bodies, whether they move in the same or in opposite directions. It is true that in that article not even the semblance of a proof is proposed. I agree that the distinction between quantity and determination of motion is correct, and that sometimes the one may be changed while the other is preserved. But, on the other hand, it happens not infrequently that they do change simultaneously, and indeed the two tend to maintain each other mutually. A body tends with all its force and all its quantity of motion to preserve its determination or direction, and as much as it loses in velocity, the direction remaining unchanged, is also lost in its determination. For, advancing more slowly in the same direction, it is less determined to preserve it. Moreover, if the body A strikes the body B, of smaller mass and at rest, it will continue in the same direction though with diminished motion; if it strikes the body B, of equal mass and at rest, it will stop, so that while A is at rest its movement is communicated to B. Finally if A strikes B, either at rest and of greater mass, or of equal mass but moving in the opposite direction, then it is evident that A will be reflected. Whence it follows that a greater opposition is needed to throw back A in a direction opposite to its original one than to reduce it to rest; this, too, invalidates Descartes' contention. For the opposition is greater when the opposing body is greater or when it moves with greater force in the opposite direction.

Descartes also contends that movement, as a simple thing,

perseveres until it is destroyed by an external cause; I agree with this, not only with regard to the quantity of movement, but also with regard to its determination. And the determination itself, that is, the moving body's force of progressing, has its own quantity—a quantity which it is easier to diminish than to reduce to zero, that is, to rest; and easier (that is, requiring less opposition to be overcome) to stop and reduce to rest than to make return backward, that is, to impart to the body the opposite motion. This we have just pointed out above. Thus it is true that movement in general is not contrary to movement, yet actual movement opposes itself to actual movement in the opposite direction, or progression to the opposite progression. The cause of this is, as we have shown, that less change and less opposition are necessary to diminish the progression than to abolish it completely and to transform it into regression. Descartes' reasoning here seems to me to resemble that of a man who would argue that in the shock of two bodies they can never break or fall into parts but only bend and mutually adjust their figures, and who would prove this by saying that matter is different from figure and that matter cannot be opposed to matter but only figure to figure. Furthermore, such an argument would claim that the quantity of matter can be preserved in a body while the figure changes. From all this he would conclude that the figure alone must be changed by the shock, since a body can never be reduced in magnitude. Descartes certainly would have proposed different laws of motion had the following consideration occurred to him. When a body strikes another body and is reflected, it first must slow down its progression, then stop, and only then return backward; thus it does not pass from one determination to the opposite by a jump, but gradually. For it should be noted that any body, however hard, is nonetheless to a certain degree flexible and resilient, like a blown-up ball which, when it falls to the floor or when a rock is thrown on it, flattens or is indented a little bit until the force of the shock or of the progression is gradually broken and finally subsides; then the ball resumes its form, shakes off the rock which no longer resists, or rebounds from the floor on which it has fallen.

Something similar happens in all repercussion, although the deformation and resumption of form cannot be observed by the eye; it is, however, clearly verified by experiments. But Descartes, all too certain of his lasting glory, has manifested in his letters only supercilious contempt for the explanation of reflection by elastic force, which Hobbes had first proposed.[15] We need not examine again the argument by which he undertook to demonstrate in article 42 the second part of this alleged law of nature, namely, that in the shock of two bodies the one loses as much movement as the other gains. For we have already shown apropos of article 36 that Descartes' supposition that the quantity of motion must always remain the same is altogether erroneous.

45. *The means of determining how much any one body's motion is changed through the impact of other bodies, according to the following rules.*

On Article 45. Before I come to the scrutiny of the special rules of motion proposed by our author, I want to give a general criterion, *quasi* a touchstone, on which they can be tested; I want to call it the *Law of Continuity.* I have explained it some time ago in another place,[16] but I wish to come back to it here with greater detail, as follows. When two hypothetical conditions or two different data continually approach each other until finally the one of them passes into the other, then necessarily also the results sought or the effects of both conditions must continually approach each other and the one finally must disappear into the other and vice versa. Take as an example an ellipse, one focus of which remains unmoved while the other

[15] See the discussion between Descartes and Hobbes on elasticity, Adam-Tannery, III, 287, 300, 313, 318.

[16] *Lettre de M. L. sur un principe général utile à l'explication des loix de la nature par la considération de la sagesse divine, pour servir de replique à la réponse du R. P. Malebranche (Letter of M. Leibniz on a General Principle Useful for the Explanation of the Laws of Nature by the Consideration of the Divine Wisdom, to Serve as a Reply to the Response of the Reverend Father Malebranche)*, 1687 (*Philosophische Schriften*, Gerhardt edn., III, 51).

moves farther and farther away, the perpendicular axis remaining all the time of the same length: then new ellipses will result which will continually approach a parabola and ultimately will become completely parabolic, namely, when the distance of the moving focus from the unmoved focus will have become immense. Therefore the properties of these ellipses, as well, will more and more approach those of the parabola, so that eventually the properties of the former will be identical with those of the latter, and the parabola can be considered as an ellipse the second focus of which is infinitely distant. Hence all the properties of the ellipse in general will also be verifiable of the parabola considered as such an ellipse. Geometry is full of examples of this kind. But the same is the case in nature, the supremely wise Author of which applies the most perfect geometry. If this were not the case there could not be any orderly course of natural events. Thus, continually diminishing movement finally evanesces into rest, and continually diminishing inequality passes into exact equality; hence rest may be considered as infinitely small movement or infinite slowness and equality as infinitely small inequality. This is the reason why all that is true of movement in general or of inequality in general applies, according to this interpretation, also to rest or equality. By this means the rules of rest or equality can in a way be conceived as special cases of the rules of movement or inequality. If this is unsuccessful it may be taken for granted that the rules are incorrect and badly conceived. We shall later show apropos of article 53 how if a line is drawn representing the variations of the hypothetical conditions, a line representing the variations of the results must correspond, while the rules of Descartes produce a monstrous and inconsistent diagram.

46 *to* 52. *Rules* 1 *to* 7.

On Article 46. Let us look now at Descartes' rules of movement. The bodies are supposed in all that follows to be hard, and unhampered by any conditions other than those stated.

RULE 1. If *B* and *C* are equal in mass and velocity and collide directly, both will be reflected with the velocity they had before the shock.

This first Cartesian rule of movement is the only one which is perfectly sure. The demonstration is as follows: Since the condition of the two bodies is equal, either both will continue their movement and will penetrate each other, which is absurd; or both will come to rest, but then their power would be lost; or both will be reflected and that with their former velocity, because if the velocity of the one were diminished, then the velocity of the other would also have to diminish because of the parity of conditions on both sides. But if the velocity of both were diminished, the sum total of forces would also be diminished, which cannot happen.

On Article 47. RULE 2. If *B* and *C* collide with the same velocity but *B* has the larger mass, then only *C* will be reflected and *B* will continue, both will retain the former velocity, and thus both will move together in the direction which *B* had before the shock.

This rule is false and inconsistent with the first, as appears by the criterion proposed above. For if the inequality, that is to say, the excess of *B* over *C*, is continually diminished until it passes into full equality, the results, too, must approach the result of equality. Suppose, therefore, that *B*, striking *C*, which comes from the opposite direction, overpowers *C*, due to an excess sufficiently great to let *B* continue its progression after the shock: then if the mass of *B* should be gradually diminished, its progression must also be gradually diminished, until a certain ratio between *B* and *C* is reached, so that *B* will come to a full stop. If *B* is then diminished still further, its movement will turn in the opposite direction and will gradually increase, until finally, when all inequality between *B* and *C* has disappeared, the rule of equality will enter into action; then, after the shock, according to Rule 1, the reflected movement of *B* will be equal to its movement before the shock. This second rule of Descartes, therefore, cannot be vindicated. For suppose the mass of *B* to be continually diminished, approaching the mass of *C* until the difference is so small that it becomes almost unrecognizable; yet if we believe Descartes, the results of equality and inequality between B and C would remain always widely different and would not approach each other gradually. However small the excess of B over C, B will always continue moving in the same direction with the same velocity; consequently, when the excess disappears, suddenly a great jump would have to occur in the results, although the given conditions would have varied only very slightly. Finally, indeed—namely, when the indefinitely small difference between B and C disappears and thus the two bodies become equal—B would have to pass suddenly from its however small forward movement to a however small backward movement, jumping over all the infinite number of intermediate cases. Thus it would happen that in two cases in which the difference of hypothetical conditions or of what is given is infinitely small, that is, less than any given quantity, the results, nevertheless, will differ very much and very noticeably. The two cases, therefore, will approach each other instantaneously and only in the last moment of the passage into equality. They will begin and cease to approach each other at the same instant, namely, when they coincide, which is contrary to reason. A consequence of this situation would also be that the rule concerning equality, that is, infinitely small inequality, could not be subsumed under the general rule of inequality. When B and C, equal in mass and velocity, strike each other, according to Rule 1 both are reflected with their former velocity. Therefore, if the mass of B is slightly increased or that of C slightly decreased (that of B remaining unchanged), the effect also must change and approach slightly the effect which would obtain through the greatest possible diminution of C, that is, its complete suppression. We are here considering, however, the case when C begins to diminish only slightly below B. In this case we will be unable to begin passing from the case of complete equality and hence complete reflection to the case of the greatest inequality, that is, the complete suppression of C, and hence the unchanged progression of B, otherwise than by beginning to diminish the reflection of B. If, hereafter, the difference between B and C is gradually increased, an excess of B will finally be reached such that B will not be reflected at all but will stop as if hesitating midway between progression and regression. If then the excess of B is further increased, it will clearly continue moving in the direction it had before the shock. It is true that the mass of B can never be increased to the extent that the velocity of its forward movement would not be slightly diminished by the opposite movement of C, unless the ratio between B and C became infinite, that is, C completely disappeared. This is how two bodies of unequal mass but equal velocity, coming from opposite directions and striking each other, behave in truth; and this rule is conformable to reason and self-consistent. Here we need not determine precisely the velocities of the two bodies after the shock. This determination requires more thorough research and I have dealt with it elsewhere in greater detail.[17]

On Article 48. RULE 3. If B and C are of equal mass and, coming from opposite directions with unequal velocities, collide, then B, which has the greater velocity, will drive before it the slower C and, losing half the difference of the two velocities, will communicate it to C, so that after the shock both will proceed together with equal velocity.

This rule is no less false than the preceding nor less incompatible with reason and experience. For, to apply our criterion, let us admit the hypothesis that the faster body B will drive before it the slower body C, as has been claimed above, and that the velocity of B will continually decrease until the velocities of both bodies become equal or, which comes to the same, until the excess of the velocity of B over that of C becomes infinitely small. Then both will move together, with the former velocity of B not diminished by any assignable quantity—which is absurd, and contrary to the first rule. For this first rule correctly stated that in the case of complete equality of masses and veloci-

17 *Dynamica de potentia et legibus naturae corporeae* (*The Dynamics of Power and of the Laws of Corporeal Nature*) (*Mathematische Schriften*, Gerhardt edn., VI, 281).

ties, or even when the differences of masses or velocities are smaller than any assignable quantity, both bodies will be reflected with their previous velocities or with this velocity increased or diminished only by an unassignable quantity. It is also impossible that the result of evanescent inequality should not pass insensibly into the result of equality.

On Article 49. RULE 4. If *B*, which is moving, is smaller than *C*, which is at rest, *B* will be reflected with the velocity it had before the shock while *C* will remain at rest.

What is sure in this rule is this, that the smaller body will always be reflected when meeting a larger body at rest; but its velocity will not be the same which it had before the shock, for the more the excess of *C* decreases, the more the repulsion will decrease, until finally the case of equality is reached and Rule 6 applies. It is absurd to maintain that when the hypothetical conditions gradually approach the case of the equality of the bodies, the results should not also gradually approach this case, but remain always the same up to the point at which they pass instantaneously, as if by a jump, into the case of equality. One will easily understand that it is also contrary to reason that when the hypothetical conditions vary continuously, the results should not vary at all, except in a single determined case. This would be contrary to all the examples which show that when the hypothetical conditions vary, the results must vary, except in particular cases, when perhaps diverse variations combine to compensate each other mutually.

On Article 50. RULE 5. If *B*, larger than *C* and in motion, strikes *C*, at rest, then *B* will continue to move and the two bodies will move together with equal velocity, but with the quantity of motion they had before the shock.

This rule, too, is erroneous. It fails to determine the true measure of velocity for both bodies, affirming that after the shock they move together; but this can never happen in the shock of hard bodies. It is, however, correct that a larger body striking a smaller at rest continues to move after the shock. But our criterion also makes it clear that in the present case they cannot move together, for let B be however little larger than C, and C however little smaller than B—we have then two cases which can approach each other until their difference becomes unrecognizably small: it cannot happen, therefore, that the results of the two cases be separated by a wide gap. But this would happen if, in the first case, they continued together in the direction which B had before the shock while, in the latter case, B would be reflected in the opposite direction with all its former velocity.

On Article 51. RULE 6. If B and C are equal, B moving while C is at rest, then B will be reflected with three-quarters of the velocity with which it came, while C will move in the former direction of B with the remaining quarter of the velocity of B.

So says Descartes. But I wonder whether in this matter anything could be thought out which would be more alien to reason, and I am highly astonished that such an idea could occur to so great a mind. But let the Cartesians worry about the justification of the master's doctrine; it will be sufficient for us to demonstrate the inconsistency of his rules. If B and C are equal and collide with equal velocities, according to Rule 1 both B and C will be reflected with their previous velocities. Now let the velocity of C be continuously diminished while the velocity of B remains unchanged, then necessarily B will be reflected with a diminished velocity and C with an increased velocity; for what the one of the two equal bodies loses in velocity will be added to the velocity of the other. Now suppose the velocity of C to evanesce, that is, let C come to a stop; then let us ask how much velocity will be lost by the reflected body B. Rule 6 of Descartes claims that B will lose only a quarter of its original velocity. Going one step further, let us now suppose that the mass of the resting body C be somewhat diminished; then, according to Rule 5, B will continue moving. Thus a minimal variation of the effect, that is, a jump, will be produced. Indeed, when C was at rest and equal to B, B was reflected with great velocity, namely three-quarters of its initial velocity; while now, however little the mass of C be diminished, the reflected movement of B will be entirely destroyed, in fact, what is more, converted into its opposite, namely, into a continuation of its original movement. This means jumping over all the intermediate cases, which is absurd. Hence it must be stated that if B and C are equal and if C is at rest before the shock, B will come to rest after the shock and will communicate its whole velocity to C. This conclusion can also be drawn from what is sure in Rules 4 and 5, for according to Rule 4 if B strikes C, resting and of greater mass, B will always be reflected; according to Rule 5, on the contrary, if B strikes C, resting and of lesser mass, B will always continue its movement. Therefore if B strikes C, at rest and of equal mass, B will neither continue its movement nor be reflected, but the result will be the mean of these two cases, that is, B will come to a stop and communicate its whole force to C.

On Article 52. RULE 7. Suppose that B and C move in the same direction, B moving behind C with a greater velocity and C moving ahead of B but with a lesser velocity; suppose, furthermore, that C is greater than B but that the ratio of the masses C and B is lesser than the ratio of the velocities of B and C; then the two bodies will continue together their movement in the same direction with a velocity which would leave the former quantity of motion unchanged. If, on the contrary, C is larger than B and the ratio of the masses of C and B is greater than the ratio of the velocities of B and C, B will be reflected with its former velocity and C will continue its movement with its former velocity.

This is what our author affirms, but it will be easily understood how absurd his contention is. For we have already remarked that hard bodies (as we suppose them here) never stay together after the shock, which is exactly what in the first case would happen here. And nothing is more alien to reason than that, when B acts on C, *it does not alter C at all, while B suffers a very considerable modification,* which happens indeed in the second case. These statements, if I am not mistaken, are a challenge to a metaphysics which may be called natural and which is revealed to us by the light of reason. There are in this rule also other inconsistencies with the former one. For let the excess of the mass of C over B be infinitely small, which is the case of equality, and let C move ahead of B with infinitely small velocity, that is, be at rest, then we have a case falling under the first part of Rule 7. The conclusion would have to be that the two bodies after the shock will move together—while it follows from what we have said apropos of Rule 6, that B will be reduced to rest and communicate its total force to C, which was at rest before the shock and of equal mass with B. For brevity's sake I shall pass in silence over other equally serious inconsistencies. But finally I must call attention to the fact that our author has forgotten to mention the intermediary case in which the ratios of the masses and of the velocities are inversely proportional; and it does not seem possible to decide for this case under the present rule. For the effect of this condition would also have to be midway between the two cases of Rule 7 and be situated in the vicinity of both. But though *the first and the second case of the rule stand close to each other as to the hypothetical conditions, their effects are widely distant,* which again conflicts with our criterion. Descartes has also said nothing concerning the case when B has a larger mass than C. He would have had to add a Rule 8 to explain what happens when two unequal bodies, coming from opposite directions, with unequal velocities, collide. He would also have had to distinguish between the central and the eccentric shock, and between the perpendicular and the oblique shock. With this we must end our criticism, not wishing to insist any longer on a discredited and regrettable doctrine.

53. *That the application of these rules is difficult, because every body is simultaneously in contact with many others.*

On Article 53. Descartes recognized that it is difficult to apply his rules, since he saw that they are completely refuted by experience. In the true rules of motion there is, on the contrary, a wonderful harmony between reason and experience; and the success of the true rules is not hampered by the surrounding bodies as much as he seemed to fear, in order to leave himself an opening for escape. In truth, the greater the mass and the hardness of the bodies, the more accurately observations will confirm the rules. We will soon show the difference in this respect between solid and liquid bodies. At this point I wish to facilitate understanding by illustrating in a figure how, with the help of our criterion, an outline of the truth can be presented in anticipation of and *quasi* a sort of prelude to a perfect delineation of the truth which may be obtained later: a very useful device both for recognizing errors and for approaching truth.

Let us suppose, therefore, that the bodies B and C are equal and that the velocity and direction of B are represented by the straight line BW, so that the movement of B tends from B toward W with a velocity BW. Suppose, furthermore, that the velocity and direction of C be variable and represented by the lines AH, so that in the cases AH_1 or AH_2 (H being below A) the direction of C be the same as that of B. Thus in the case AH_1, equal to BW, the velocity of both is equal and the direction the same, but if H is put closer to A, as in H_2, the direction of C from A toward H_2 is the same as that of B, namely BW, while the velocity of C is less than that of B because AH_2 is shorter than BW; in this case, C moving ahead of B can be struck by B. If H coincides with A, as in H_3, then the direction and velocity of C are zero, that is, C is at rest. If, however, H is put above A, as in H_4, H_5, H_6, then C moves in a direction opposite to B. Let us draw now the lines PP and QQ so that the ordinate HP represents the velocity and direction of B after the shock, and HQ the velocity and direction of C after the shock; be it furthermore understood that the direction of one of them, or of both, which after the shock is the same as the direction of B before the shock, be represented by application to the left, while the opposite direction be represented by application to the right.

Let us now determine some points on the lines PP and QQ. The direction and velocity—in a word, the movement—of B

before the shock is always BW: let now the movement of C before the shock be equal to that of B and in the same direction, namely AH_1 (equal to BW); then the two bodies B and C, notwithstanding their contact, will both retain their former velocities and directions. Therefore the two lines H_1P_1 and H_1Q_1, which represent the movements of B and C after the shock, will be equal to AH_1 and to BW, and to the left. But when the movement of C before the shock is zero or AH_3 (the point H_3 coinciding with A), that is, when C is at rest, then also the result is evident: after the shock the body B will come to rest; therefore the point P_3 will coincide with A, while C will acquire the velocity and direction which B had before. We obtain then H_3Q_3, equal to BW and to the left and, thus, the points P_3 and Q_3 are determined. Finally, if the movement of C is equal to that of B but in the opposite direction, it will have to be represented by AH_5 equal to BW but H_5 situated above A. That is to say if the supposed bodies (assumed to be equal) meet with equal velocities but coming from opposite directions, the result can also be seen in our diagram: each of the two bodies will be reflected with its previous velocity, and thus the points P_5 and Q_5 will be obtained. For H_5P_5 will again be equal to BW, but to the right, for thus B is reflected, that is, moved in the direction opposite to its previous one; and H_5Q_5 will also be equal to BW, but to the left, because C now moves in the direction which B had before. Hence, we obtain the points P_1, P_3, P_5 which, as should be noticed, lie on a straight line, as well as the points Q_1, Q_3, Q_5 which lie on another straight line parallel to AH. The other points, e.g., P_2, P_4, P_6, etc., or Q_2, Q_4, Q_6, cannot be determined by our criterion alone, namely, by the law of continuity; that is, the lines PP and QQ cannot be deduced from this law. It is sufficient to connect by a continuous line all the cases to which our criterion applies. By this means all these inconsistent rules of Descartes may be eliminated even before the matter is fully known or the species of line discovered. Meanwhile, we know from elsewhere that these lines PP and QQ are indeed straight lines and that HP is always equal to AH, and HQ to BW, because of the permutation of

According to Descartes—a bizarre scheme

According to the truth—a regular scheme

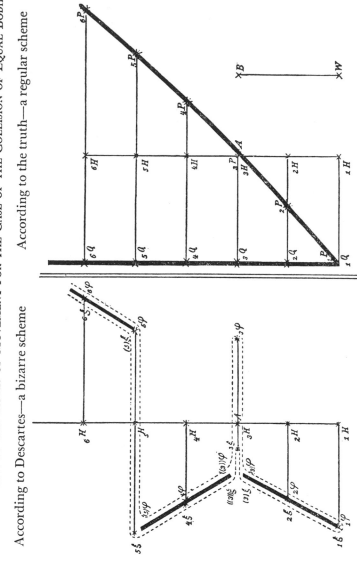

66

Before the shock

the movement of the body B is BW (constant), of the body C, A_1H, A_2H, etc.

After the shock

the movement of B is

for Descartes: $H_1\varphi$, $H_2\varphi$, etc.

    for us: H_1P, H_2P, etc.

the movement of C is

for Descartes: HQ (constant).

    for us: $H_1\xi$, $H_2\xi$, etc.

H below [above] A

$P\}$

$\varphi\}$ to the left [right] of AH $\Big\}$ signify the same [the opposite] direction in relation to the direction B had before the shock.

$Q\}$

$\xi\}$

$_1\varphi$	$_2\varphi$	$_{(3)}\varphi$,	$_1\xi$	$_2\xi$	$_3\xi$	according to Descartes' rule 7.
$_{((3))}\varphi$	$_4\varphi$	$_{(5)}\varphi$,	$_{((3))}\xi$	$_4\xi$	$_5\xi$	according to Descartes' rule 3.
		$_3\varphi$,			$_3\xi$	according to Descartes' rule 6.
		$_5\varphi$,			$_5\xi$	according to Descartes' rule 1.

Our diagram and the Cartesian agree on two cases only, H_1 and H_5, out of an infinite number. Our diagram obeys the Law of Continuity, the Cartesian shows discontinuity and leaps, in the line $\varphi\varphi$ in $_3\varphi$ and $_5\varphi$, in the line $\xi\xi$ in $_3\xi$ and $_5\xi$. The leap is marked by points to represent continuity. It is impossible to except from the coincidence of two continuous lines, $\varphi\varphi$ and $\xi\xi$, a determinate number of points, e.g., two, so that all points φ coincide with all the corresponding points ξ, except in two cases, namely $_3\varphi$ with $_3\xi$, and $_5\varphi$ with $_5\xi$. Yet this is what must happen in the Cartesian diagram.

$_{(3)}\varphi$ and $_{((3))}\varphi$ ought to coincide in $_3\varphi$

$\left.\begin{array}{l} _{(5)}\varphi \\ _5\xi \end{array}\right\}$ ought to coincide with $\left\{\begin{array}{l} _5\varphi \\ _{(5)}\xi \end{array}\right.$

velocities and directions in the case of equal bodies. Therefore, HQ as well as BW can be considered here as constant and representing at the same time movements in the same direction. For the rest, I do not determine the points below H_1, P_1, Q_1, because in these cases the velocity of B would be inferior to that of C, that is, B could not catch up with C and their shock would be impossible.

In the same way, one could construct a graph for the case of bodies with equal velocities, where one of them would remain of constant mass while that of the other would vary. In this case, too, the results of their shocks could be represented by two lines, and a similar figure could be traced for any hypothetical condition, provided that, with the exception of one variable, they remain constant. But the specimen produced for one case may suffice, the more so since, using a different method, we have attained complete knowledge of what has only been outlined in this context. But we have shown that the method used here at least has its use for refuting errors. Even though all the rules had not yet been discovered, this method would help us to anticipate them. The Cartesian rules, on the contrary, do not allow the drawing of a continuous line representing the varied results, which would correspond to the continuous line of varying hypothetical conditions. If the Cartesian rules are delineated, the product is entirely malformed and contrary to our criterion proposed in the remarks on article 45, that is, to the *Law of Continuity*. I have therefore confronted in a figure the delineations of our and of the Cartesian doctrines, thus rendering visible the inconsistency, or rather the impossibility, of the latter.

54. *The difference between hard and fluid bodies.* —55. *The parts of hard bodies are united by no other cement than their motionlessness.*

On Articles 54, 55. There is some truth, but also much error, in Descartes' theory that bodies are *fluid* when their particles are agitated by various motions in all directions, *hard* when their parts are mutually at relative rest, and that no other *glue* holds matter together but the motionlessness of one part with respect to the other. Descartes concludes thus that hardness, or, as I prefer to call it with a more general term, *firmness* (which, to a certain degree, is present also in soft bodies) has rest as its sole cause; he reaches this conclusion by arguing that the glue which causes the cohesion cannot be a body (otherwise the same question would come up again). Hence, this cause must be, as he correctly affirms, a mode of the body. But there is no mode of the body more apt to produce this effect than rest, he thinks. Why that? Because rest is the mode of the body most opposed to movement. I am astonished that Descartes arrived at such a conclusion by such weak and superficial, even sophistic, reasoning. In syllogistic form, it would run as follows: Rest is a mode of the body most opposed to movement; now, the mode of the body most opposed to movement is the cause of firmness. *Ergo*, rest is the cause of firmness. But both premises are false, though they have some slight appearance of truth. It happens all too frequently in Descartes, that he takes the most uncertain things for the most certain and satisfies the superficial reader by his dictatorial briefness; for example, when he concludes that extension constitutes matter, that thought is independent of matter, and that the same quantity of motion is conserved in nature. In all these cases the authoritative style is more effective than the strength of the arguments. As for myself, I think that the opposite movement is more contrary to a given movement than rest, and that a greater opposition is needed to impart to a body a movement in the direction opposite to that from which it came than to bring it to a stop, as I have proved apropos of article 47. But proof is also required for the second premise of the syllogism, namely, that the cause of firmness is what is most opposed to movement. Perhaps the author had the following prosyllogism in mind: Firmness is most opposed to movement; whatever is most opposed to movement, the cause thereof is also most opposed to movement. But again both premises of this prosyllogism are very weak indeed. I deny that firmness is most opposed to movement; I concede only that firmness is most opposed to the movement of one part without the others, and this is precisely the phenomenon the cause of which has to be discovered. I also doubt the certainty of the principle: what is most opposed to a thing, the cause thereof also is most opposed to that thing. What could be more opposed to death than life? And yet who would deny that the cause of an animal's death very often is a living being? On such vague philosophical principles for which the limits of application have not yet been established no demonstration can be based.

Some readers will blame us for trying to send such great philosophers back to school with our syllogisms; others may despise objections so trite. But I have found that those great philosophers, not to speak of other men, often fail in matters of greatest consequence due to neglect of this elementary logic, and that this is even the most frequent cause of their errors. Indeed, what else is contained in this logic than the most general commands of supreme reason, formulated in easily understandable rules? I have thought it opportune to show once by this example, how useful it is to put an argument into the prescribed form in order to show its value, particularly when imagination is unable to succor reason, as it can do in mathematics, and when we have to deal with an author whose reasoning on great problems runs in precipitous arguments.

Since, therefore, the reasons proposed by Descartes are of no avail for the problem under discussion, it is convenient to return to the investigation of the thing itself. What is to be considered in firmness is not so much rest but the force by which one part pulls another with it. Let A and B be two perfect cubes, at rest relative to each other and having perfectly polished faces: let the cube B be situated at the left of cube A, one face of B covering one face of A, so that no interval is left between them. Now a little ball C strikes cube A in the middle, in a direction parallel to the coincident faces. Thus the shock will not be communicated to cube B, unless the latter is supposed to be attached to cube A. Under these conditions it is true that A, by its rest, will resist the shock of C and can be propelled by C

only if C loses some of its force; therefore it is also true that in this case the rest of A opposes its separation from B. But this effect is only accidental: it is not produced because the shock tends to separate A from B, but because A has to absorb the force of the shock, and the same would happen if B were not present at all. Once A has received the shock, it will go its way and leave B behind, just as though the latter never had been next to it. It is a sophism, therefore, to infer from the fact that both A and B preserve their conditions as much as possible, that two bodies at rest with regard to one another stick to each other and that their firmness is the effect of their mere motionlessness. With equal right it might be inferred that two bodies at ten feet distance from each other are linked together and tend to preserve always this same distance. Hence what must be explained is this: why there sometimes is cohesion between two cubes A and B, so that they form a solid parallelepiped the whole of which is put into movement when A only is pushed; in other words, why cube A when pushed pulls cube B with it. What is required here is to discover the cause of traction in nature. There are certain eminent scientists who affirm perfect unity itself to be the cause of firmness, an explanation which seems to satisfy several partisans of atomism. Suppose the parallelepiped AB to be an atom, which the mind can divide into those two cubes A and B but which actually is not divided; then, they say, this atom will not actually be divisible either, but will always remain one solid. There are many objections to this, the first being that they propose no demonstration of their thesis. Let us suppose that two atoms, D and E, simultaneously run against the parallelepiped AB, so that their forward faces cover the cubes A and B, respectively, and that the directions of their movements are parallel to the common face of the cubes A and B; let D come from behind, from F, and collide with its whole face with the congruent whole face of A and similarly let E come from the front, from G, and collide with B: The question then is, why A is not driven away from B, toward G, and why B is not driven away from A, in the

opposite direction, toward F. No reason for this is offered in
the theory of the atomists. What is the difference, indeed, between saying that A and B form a unit and saying that they are
not actually divided? If you answer, as certain scholars do, that
before the actual division there are no parts in the continuum,
then the following alternative emerges: either this principle
does not oppose division when a cause supervenes which tends
to actualize the division and which, so to speak, designates or
distinguishes the parts (as for instance the shock of D and E);
or else no continuum could ever be broken into parts. What
would happen, then, when the two cubic atoms A and B, which
were separate before, approach each other to the point where
one face of the one would coincide with one face of the other?
Would there be any difference at all, in the moment of contact,
between the two atoms and the one atom in the form of a
parallelepiped AB which has been described a while ago? If the
hypothesis just mentioned were true, two atoms would stick
together and the simple contact would act like a sort of glue;
the same effect should be produced even if only parts of the
faces coincided. Hence it would follow that, due to a natural
progression, the atoms should continually grow like a snowball
rolling in the snow; one would then have to expect all matter
to coalesce into a single body harder than diamond and to end
in eternal immobility. For the cause of the coalescence would
subsist while no cause for dissolution would emerge. Those who
hold this opinion have only one means of escaping this consequence: namely, to object that in nature there are no perfectly
plane surfaces or, if there were any, they would cease to exist
due to this very coalescence; moreover, all atoms are enclosed
within curved surfaces which are absolutely unable to adjust to
each other. This would doubtless be true if all atoms were
spherical. For then there could be no contact between them
along an entire surface. But let us set aside the impossibility of
presenting a valid reason for excluding from nature bodies
terminated by plane surfaces, or, at any rate, by surfaces which
can coincide with others. Yet we again ask the atomists for a
reason why the continuum should not be divisible into parts.

We could propose still other very important arguments against atoms, but we do not propose to exhaust the matter here.

Others explain the hardness of bodies by the same cause which makes it very difficult to separate two polished tablets, namely that the surrounding air opposes the separation, that is, the air cannot penetrate instantaneously into the interval between the tablets, which would be created by this separation. Thus, according to this theory, hardness would be the effect of compression. In many cases this is correct. Yet compression cannot be the general cause of hardness, since it presupposes the existence of a certain hardness or firmness, namely that of the tablets themselves. Nor does it help to say that the cubes A and B are held together by some kind of cement, for this would presuppose a certain firmness of the cement, due to which the parts of it would themselves be held together and stick to the two bodies united by cement. One could also conceive little spines of A fitting into little holes of B and likewise little spines of B fitting into little holes of A. Thus one of the two bodies could not be moved without the other unless these appendages be broken. But then a new question would arise, namely, what is the cause of the firmness of these appendages?

Ignoring all these hypotheses which either are useless or do not solve the problem, I think that the primordial cause of cohesion is motion, I mean conspiring motion. (It is evident that impenetrability itself must be added, when the body has no place to yield or when there is no reason why it should yield to one impact rather than to another. Thus a perfect sphere rotating in a milieu which is a plenum, homogeneous, and at rest, is prevented from emitting anything through its centrifugal force.) I suggest that matter which is in itself homogeneous and homogeneously divisible is diversified only by motion. And we see, indeed, that even liquids acquire a certain firmness through motion. Thus a powerful jet of water will oppose the intrusion of a foreign body into its path more forcefully than would the same water at rest. For the intrusion of an extraneous body would of necessity produce a strong disturbance of the conspiring motion of the water; but to disturb motion, that is, to change it considerably, force is necessary. Try to stick a finger into a jet of water and you will see that drops are vigorously dispersed in all directions, and therefore whatever touches the jet is somewhat repelled. But when there is some kind of matter without cohesion, similar to sand without cement, it can by motion alone acquire a certain consistency. This is done in a remarkable experiment in which a magnet is brought close to iron filings: for suddenly the iron filings arrange themselves into lines and nets, and matter seems to dispose itself as if in rows. I have no doubt that a certain kind of magnetism, that is, of internal conspiring motion, is also the agent which connects the parts of certain other bodies. Thus the primordial cause of consistency or cohesion satisfies reason as well as the senses.

56. *The particles of fluids move with equal force in all directions. A hard body put in a fluid can be determined to motion with a minimum of force.* —57. *Demonstration of the preceding article.*

On Articles 56, 57. There is no need to investigate the cause of fluidity, since matter is fluid by itself, unless there is in it some motion which is disturbed by the separation of certain parts. It is not necessary, therefore, that a fluid be agitated by diverse motions of its particles. It is, however, a well-established general law of nature that all bodies are agitated by internal motions, and it follows therefrom that they are firm when these motions are conspiring, while they remain fluid when these motions are disturbed and in no way systematically connected. Hence it follows that in every body there is a certain degree of fluidity and of firmness. Indeed, nothing is so hard that it lacks flexibility altogether, and *vice versa*. This internal motion, furthermore, is imperceptible; for the particles which continually succeed each other are very small and similar and therefore not discernible by the senses, and their motion is so rapid (like the jet of water or the spoke in a wheel) that they appear a continuous solid. The internal motion of fluids is also confirmed by the dissolution of salts in water, by the corrosions produced by acid liquids, as also in general by heat, which when it is strong produces the boiling of liquids, and when it is of medium strength, only their agitation. But when in winter the agitation produced by heat is weakened, the internal motion of the conspiring particles which is alone proper to matter, predominates in most liquids, so that they become turgid and eventually congeal. Another rough specimen of this agitation in fluids extraordinarily disturbed is offered by the dust particles which can be seen when sun rays shine into an otherwise dark room. Now in liquids which, judged by our senses, are without motion, movement can with equal ease be produced everywhere and in all directions. Hence in these liquids those disorderly motions are distributed with sufficient equality, and *quasi* compensate each other. Thus, if you put a solid body in such a liquid it will be pushed by the shocks and the waves of the fluid equally from all sides, and therefore its own motions will be neither increased nor impeded.

58. *That a body should not be considered entirely fluid in regard to a solid body which it surrounds, if some of its particles move with a velocity less than that of the solid. —59. That a solid body pushed by another solid body does not receive all the movement it acquires from the propelling body alone, but borrows part of it also from the surrounding fluid. —60. It cannot, however, acquire from that fluid a greater velocity than it has received from the propelling solid body. —61. When a fluid moves entirely in a definite direction, it carries with it necessarily any immersed solid body. —62. When a solid body is thus carried away by a fluid, it cannot properly be said to be in motion.*

On Article 59. When a body floating in a liquid is pushed by an external force, then, Descartes believes, even though this force may not be sufficient to propel the body, movement will result, nevertheless, due to the concourse of those particles of the fluid which favor this motion; moreover, the other particles will also be thereby determined to favor the motion by means of retaining their own motion while their determination or direction is changed by the force. To this add what our author says at the end of article 56 and the demonstration thereof in article 57. From this he infers that a hard body moving in a fluid does not borrow its motion totally from the propelling hard body but partly also from the fluid in which it is floating. But this he himself will soon contradict in article 60, and I consider all this as absolutely unfounded. For here again he depends upon the false principle that rest is the opposite of motion, and what he says seems to be meant exclusively to mask the contradiction of observed phenomena to our author's fourth rule. For in this rule he wrongly denies that a body at rest can be set in motion by a body of inferior mass, however great the latter's velocity (see the end of article 61). Yet he is forced to concede in article 56 that a hard body floating in a liquid can be moved by a very small force. To escape this difficulty he resorts to a strange fiction, calling to his aid the particles of the fluid—all this, of course, in vain. For since the movements of these particles are compensated by opposite movements, they can be of no avail; and if they had any effect, it would be too great for the hypothesis, for they would impart to the floating body more movement than it ought to gain from the impelling force. It is obvious, on the contrary, that in the propelled body, there is no greater movement and therefore no other movement than there would be if the fluid in which it flows were not agitated at all. It must also be stated that the fluid not only adds nothing to the motion, but rather diminishes it somewhat and slows down the velocity of the body. The cause of this lies partly in some resistance of the fluid and partly in the well-known fact that the immersion of the hard body in the liquid requires the continual displacement and setting into motion of a portion of the liquid equal in volume to the immersed body. This, of course, entails the expenditure of a certain part of the power of the moving body. I have calculated elsewhere[18] the quantity

[18] *Schediasma de resistentia medii et motu projectorum gravium in medio resistente* (*Remark on the Resistance of a Medium and the Motion of Heavy Bodies Projected Into a Resistant Medium*), 1689 (*Mathematische Schriften*, Gerhardt edn., VI, 135).

of these two kinds of resistance, the one of which is absolute and always the same in a given liquid, while the other is relative and increases with the velocity of the movement.

63. *Why certain bodies are so hard that, however small they may be, they cannot be divided with our hands.*

On Article 63. What Descartes teaches here concerning the cause of our inability to break an iron nail with our hands is amazing. He looks for a difficulty where there is none, and to a deceitful objection gives an answer of the same kind. If a body at rest can be moved by a more powerful body, then—this is the question under discussion—why is the hand unable to move part of the iron nail which is much smaller than the hand, though it be at rest, and to tear it off the other part? He makes the softness of the hand responsible for this failure, since this softness allegedly allows only part of the hand to operate on the nail, and this part which is in contact with the nail would always be smaller than the part of the nail to be ripped off. In truth this question has nothing to do with motion, for the hand easily moves not only part of the nail, but the whole nail. What we demand to know is rather why one part of the nail pulls the other with it, so that the one does not allow itself to be moved without the other. The recourse to the softness of the hand is, in this connection, useless. For if instead of the hand you take some piece of iron or stone, the parts of the nail will stick together none the less. And though a hard body is broken more easily by another hard than by a soft body, we are not asking here why or by what force the cohesion of any two parts of the nail can be overcome, but why this cohesion exists. Nor do we investigate the problem of why one of the parts can be moved, if only by a more powerful body (for this is false), but why it cannot easily be moved alone.

64. *In Physics I admit no other principles than in geometry or abstract Mathematics. Any other principle is undesirable. For through this method all natural phenomena can be explained and demonstrative certainty attained in these matters.*

On Article 64. The author concludes this second part, which deals with the general principle of material things, with advice which I think demands a restriction. For the explication of natural phenomena, he says, no other principles are needed but those drawn from abstract mathematics, that is, from the doctrine concerning magnitude, figure, and motion. And he recognizes no other matter than that which is the object of geometry. I fully agree that all particular natural phenomena could be explained mechanically if they were sufficiently explored by us, and that there is no other means of understanding the causes of material things. Yet, what must also constantly be kept in mind is that the mechanical principles themselves, that is, the general laws of nature, derive from higher principles and cannot be explained by quantity alone and by geometrical considerations. These principles, on the contrary, imply something metaphysical which is independent of notions furnished by our imagination and has to be referred to a substance which lacks extension. For besides extension and its modifications, there is inherent in matter the very force or power of action which allows the passage from metaphysics to nature and from material to immaterial things. This force has its own laws which derive not solely from those absolute and, so to speak, blind principles of necessity which prevail in mathematics, but from the principles of perfect reason. Once these higher principles have been established by general research, all natural phenomena can be accounted for and explained mechanically. Thereafter it will be quite useless to resort to the perceptions and inclinations of an *Archeus*, to *Ideae operatrices*,[19] to *substantial forms*, and even

---

[19] *Archeus*, a term employed by Paracelsus as well as by the Paracelcists (van Helmont, Robert Fludd, etc.) to designate the vital principle, the occult force which animates the individual substance and leads it to its perfection. For Fludd, see also note 20. The term *Ideae operatrices* had been invented by Jean Marcus Marci de Kronland (1595–1667), professor of medicine in Prague, in his book *Idearum operatricium idea, sive hypothesis et detectio illius occultae virtutis quae semina foecundat et ex iisdem corpora organica producit* (*An Idea of "Operative Ideas," or a Hypothesis and Disclosure of that Occult Virtue Which Fertilizes Seeds and Produces Organic Bodies from Them*), Prague, 1635.

to *souls,* as it will also be useless to appeal, in the explanation of particular phenomena of nature, to the simple will of a *deus ex machina,* universal cause of everything; this is precisely what I remember that the author of the *Philosophia Mosaica*[20] has done, misinterpreting the text of the sacred scriptures. By carefully observing these rules one will avoid extremes in philosophy and satisfy the requirements of theology as well as those of natural sciences. At the same time one will understand that in former times the Schoolmen erred not so much in dealing with the indivisible forms, but in applying this theory in places where the question concerned rather the modes and operations of substance and its forms of action, that is, when the question dealt with mechanism. Nature contains, so to speak, an empire within an empire, or a double government: the government of reason and the government of necessity, or the empire of forms and that of material particles. Just as all is full of souls, all is also full of organic bodies. These two realms remain distinct, each one being governed by its own law. Hence it is useless to search for the causes of perception and appetitions in the modifications of extension, just as it is useless to search for the causes of nutrition and other organic functions in the realm of forms or souls. But the supreme substance which is the universal cause of all things has by its infinite wisdom and power created the world in such a way that those two very different series are in mutual correspondence in the same corporeal substance and agree so perfectly that it may seem as though the one were directed by the influence of the other. Thus, if you study the necessary connection of material phenomena and the order of efficient causes, you will find that nothing happens without a cause that satisfies the imagination and nothing escapes the mathematical laws of mechanism. If, on the other hand, you

20 Robert Fludd (de Fluctibus) 1574–1637, a London physician, Paracelcist, adversary of Kepler, of Mersenne, of Gassendi, etc., attempted to reconcile theosophy with the new exact science in *Philosophia Mosaica in qua sapientia et scientia creationis et creaturarum explicatur (Mosaic Philosophy, in Which the Wisdom and Science of the Creation and of Created Things Are Explained),* Gouda, 1638.

contemplate the golden chain of ends and the sphere of forms which constitute, as it were, an intelligible world, you will recognize that, due to the perfection of the supreme author, the apexes of ethics and of metaphysics coincide so that nothing happens without supreme reason. For the same God is both the eminent form and first efficient cause and the end and ultimate reason of all things. It behooves us to worship his traces in the universe and not only to study the means whereby he acts to operate the causal mechanism of material processes, but also to meditate on the sublime ends of this admirable workmanship. We ought to recognize in God not only the architect of the material world, but also and even more the king of minds, whose intelligence has ordained everything for the best and who has created the world as the most perfect of all possible states, ruled by the wisest and most powerful monarch. Thus, combining in the study of the particular natural phenomena, the consideration of both points of view, we will promote simultaneously the purposes of practical life and the improvement of the mind, and advance in wisdom no less than in piety.

ON THE IMPROVEMENT OF METAPHYSICS, AND ON THE CONCEPT OF SUBSTANCE

Most of those scholars who take great pleasure in mathematics are obviously disgusted with metaphysics, because they find in the first clarity, in the latter only obscurity. The principal cause of this difference is, I think, that the general concepts of metaphysics, which are believed to be the best known to everyone, have become ambiguous and obscure as a result of human negligence and inconsistent thinking. The definitions usually given are not even nominal and, therefore, unfit to explain anything. This failure has doubtless contaminated the other disciplines which are dependent upon that first and architectonic philosophy. Thus, instead of lucid definitions, we are offered petty distinctions, and instead of truly universal principles, topical rules which often are invalidated by more instances than there are examples to confirm them. Yet, by a sort of necessity men currently use metaphysical terms, and flatter themselves by believing that they understand what they have learned to repeat. The true and fruitful concepts, not only of substance, but also of cause, action, relation, similitude, and of most of the other general terms, manifestly remain unknown at large. No wonder, therefore, that this prince of the sciences, traditionally named the First Philosophy, the one which Aristotle called "desired" or "searched for" (ζητουμένη) [zêtoumenê], has so far remained among the desiderata. It is true that Plato investigates the validity of concepts throughout his Dialogues. Aristotle does the same in his books commonly called metaphysical. But their efforts seem not to have been very successful. The later Platonists have fallen into verbal monstrosities, while the Aristotelians, and above all others the Schoolmen, have been interested rather in raising questions than in resolving them. In our own times also, some eminent men have applied their minds to the First Philosophy, so far without much success. It cannot be denied that Descartes has made some outstanding contributions and that it is his greatest merit to have revived the Platonic tendency to turn the mind away from the senses. Moreover, he has used advantageously the doubt of the Academic school. But, due to a certain inconsistency and to rash conclusions, he has all too soon gone beyond the goal, and has failed to distinguish what is certain from what is not. Thus he has advanced the absurd theory that extension is the essence of corporeal substance, and has had no sound understanding of the union of soul and body—all this because he has wrongly conceived of the nature of substance in general. For he has jumped, so to speak, to the solution of the most intricate questions, without having explained the concepts involved in them. Nowhere else does it appear with so much evidence how far from certainty his *Metaphysical Meditations* remain, than in the writing in which, challenged by Mersenne and others, he vainly tried to present them in a mathematical garb.[1] I realize that other philosophers of distinction, also, have tackled metaphysical problems and proposed profound thoughts; but these are so imbued with obscurity that these men appear to vaticinate rather than to demonstrate. Yet, to my mind, metaphysics needs clearness and certainty even more than mathematics; mathematical truths carry with them their proofs and confirmations—the most powerful cause of their success—while in metaphysics this advantage is lacking. This is why we need in metaphysics a peculiar method of establishing propositions, a sort of Ariadne's clue which will help us to resolve questions with as much ease as the method of Euclid, in short, a method imitating the calculus, but nevertheless evincing a clarity second not even to that of popular speech.

The importance of this new method will appear above all apropos of the *concept of substance*, of which I offer a definition so fruitful that therefrom the most fundamental truths can be derived, truths concerning even God and the essences of mind

[1] Descartes, "Reply to the Second Objections" against the *Meditations*, Adam-Tannery, VII, 160–161.

and body. Some of these truths are known, but insufficiently demonstrated; others are still unknown, but will be extremely useful for the other sciences. To give a foretaste of these results, I shall say meanwhile that the concept of *force* (*vis* or *virtus* in Latin, corresponding to *Kraft* in German), to which I have devoted the special science of *Dynamics*, sheds much light on the understanding of the true *concept of substance*. Active force, indeed, differs from mere power as commonly conceived by the Schoolmen in that the active power or faculty of the Schools is nothing but the proximate possibility of action—a possibility which, however, needs an external excitation or a stimulus to pass into action. Active force, on the contrary, contains a sort of activity, an entelechy; it is intermediate between the faculty to act and the action itself, and involves an effort (*conatus*). Thus, it is brought into operation by itself alone, requiring for this purpose no help, but merely the suppression of impediments. This may be illustrated by the example of a heavy body causing the tension of the cord on which it is suspended, or by that of a drawn bow. For although gravity and elastic force can and must be explained mechanically, by the motion of the ether, nevertheless, the ultimate reason for the motion in matter is the force impressed upon matter at its creation. This force is inherent in all matter, but because of the conflicting motions of corporeal objects it appears in nature limited and constrained in various ways. This force of action, I affirm, is inherent in all substance, and always engenders some action; that is, corporeal substance itself—and the same is true of spiritual substance—is never inactive. This does not seem to have been sufficiently understood by those who considered mere extension or else impenetrability as the essence of matter, and believed they could conceive a body at absolute rest. From my investigations it will also become evident that one created substance does not receive from another created substance the force of acting, as force itself, but only the limitation and determination of this tendency or force already pre-existing in it. For the present I shall say nothing more concerning the usefulness of this concept for the solution of the difficult problem concerning the interaction of substances.

ON THE ULTIMATE ORIGINATION
OF THE UNIVERSE[1]

November 23, 1697

Besides the World, that is, besides the aggregate of finite things, there is some dominant unit, not only as my soul is in myself, or rather as my ego itself is in my body, but manifesting a much higher reason. For the one being which dominates the universe not only rules the world, it also makes or creates it. It is superior to the world and, so to speak, beyond the world, and is therefore the ultimate reason of things. Neither in any single thing, nor in the total aggregate and series of things, can the sufficient reason for their existence be discovered. Let us suppose a book entitled *The Elements of Geometry* to have existed eternally, one edition having always been copied from the preceding: it is evident then that, although you can account for the present copy by a reference to the past copy which it reproduces, yet, however far back you go in this series of reproductions, you can never arrive at a complete examination, since you always will have to ask why at all times these books have existed, that is, why there have been any books at all and why this book in particular. What is true concerning these books is equally true concerning the diverse states of the world, for here too the following state is in some way a copy of the preceding one (although changed according to certain laws). However far you turn back to antecedent states, you will never discover in

[1] The word *originatio* in this title has sometimes been translated "origin." Leibniz would certainly not have written *originatio*—a term which is used by Quintillian and later authors in the sense of etymology—if he had wished to say *origo*. Moreover, the word origination seems to express better the active and "dynamic" character of the process by which, according to Leibniz, the possibles pass into actual existence.

any or all of these states the full reason why there is a world rather than nothing, nor why it is such as it is. You may well suppose the world to be eternal; yet what you thus posit is nothing but the succession of its states, and you will not find the sufficient reason in any one of them, nor will you get any nearer to accounting rationally for the world by taking any number of them together: the reason must therefore be sought elsewhere. Things eternal may have no cause of existence, yet a reason for their existence must be conceived. Such a reason is, for immutable things, their very necessity or essence; while in the series of changing things, even though this series itself may be supposed a priori to be eternal,[2] this reason would consist in the very prevailing of inclinations, as will become clear soon. For in this case reasons do not necessitate (that is, operate with absolute or metaphysical necessity, so that the contrary would imply contradiction), but only incline. Hence it is evident that even by supposing the world to be eternal, the recourse to an ultimate cause of the universe beyond this world, that is, to God, cannot be avoided.

The reasons for the world are therefore concealed in some entity outside the world, which is different from the chain or series of things, the aggregate of which constitutes the world. Thus we must pass from the physical or hypothetical necessity, which determines the later states of the world by the earlier, to something endowed with absolute or metaphysical necessity, for which no reason can be given. For the actually existing world is necessary only physically or hypothetically, but not absolutely or metaphysically. Suppose the world to be indeed in a determinate state now; then other determinate states will be necessarily engendered by it. Since therefore the ultimate root of the world must be in something which exists of metaphysical necessity, and since furthermore the reason for any existent can be only another existent, it follows that a unique entity must exist of

2 The Latin text as it appears in Erdmann and in Gerhardt is corrupted here. The correction after the Hanover manuscript follows: Gerhardt, *Philosophische Schriften*, VII, 302: line 21, for *debet* read *deberet;* line 22, for *a priore* read *a priori;* line 23, for *intelligetur* read *intelligeretur.*

metaphysical necessity, that is, that there is a being whose essence implies existence. Hence there exists a being which is different from the plurality of beings, that is, from the world; for it has been granted and proved that the world does not exist of metaphysical necessity.

But let us explain somewhat more distinctly how, from the eternal or essential—that is, metaphysical—truths, the temporal or contingent—that is, physical—truths are derived. First we must recognize this: from the fact that something rather than nothing exists, it follows that in possible things, or in their possibility or essence itself, there is a certain demand or (so to speak) a claim for existence; in short, that essence tends by itself toward existence. From this it follows, furthermore, that everything possible, that is, all that expresses a possible essence or reality, tends with equal right toward existence, the degree of this tendency being proportionate to the quantity of essence or reality, that is, to the degree of perfection of the possible involved. Perfection, indeed, is nothing else but the quantity of essence.

From this it must be concluded that, out of the infinite number of combinations and series of possibles, one exists through which a maximum of essence of possibles is produced into existence. For in all things there is a principle of determination which must be drawn from the consideration of maxima or minima, namely, that the maximum effect must be attained with a minimum of expenditure. In this respect, time and space—in short, the receptivity or capacity of the world—may be regarded as the expenditure or the area allotted for the erection of the most advantageous construction; while the variety of forms in the world represents the comfort of the building and the multitude and beauty of its rooms. The problem is analogous to that arising in certain games, in which all the squares of a board have to be filled according to given rules: if you do not use a certain skill, you eventually will find yourself excluded from certain squares and forced to leave more spaces empty than you could and should have. There is, however, a method by which a maximum number of squares can be filled with ease and certainty.[3] Or suppose, for instance, that it is decreed that a triangle be constructed, without any further determining condition being added: consequently, an equilateral triangle will be produced.[4] Or suppose that from one given point a second point has to be reached, without any further condition to determine the path: the easiest or the shortest way will be taken. So also, once it be established that being prevails over nonbeing, that is, that there is a reason why there exists something rather than nothing, or (which comes to the same) that mere possibility has to pass into actuality—this established, without any further determinations being offered: it follows that the maximum compatible with the capacity of time and place (that is, with the order of possible existence) does exist. The procedure is the same as in the game mentioned a while ago, where the greatest possible number of pieces have to be placed in a given area.

It will become admirably clear from this how, in the very origination of the universe, a sort of Divine Mathematics or a Metaphysical Mechanism is used, and how determination

[3] Leibniz was very much interested in the application of mathematics, particularly of the method of maxima and minima, to the theory of games. See the references in Couturat, *La logique de Leibniz* (*The Logic of Leibniz*), pp. 242-243. See also the discussion of the *ludus aggerum* in Leibniz' correspondence with Jakob Bernoulli (*Mathematische Schriften*, Gerhardt edn., III, 94).

[4] Leibniz seems to have forgotten here to set the condition: "a triangle of a given perimeter." In that case, the equilateral triangle is in fact the one which has the greatest surface. Compare *Tentamen anagogicum* (*Anagogical Essay*) (*Philosophische Schriften*, Gerhardt edn., VII, 278): "Suppose that nature had been obliged to construct a triangle, and that for this result only the perimeter, or the sum of the sides, had been given, nothing more; she would construct an equilateral triangle." It is quite possible that in our text, Leibniz wished to present an example not of determination by a maximum, but of a maximum of determination. In the *Tentamen anagogicum*—which is the most important and the most explicit text on the principle which was to give birth to the *principle of least action*—he completes the principle of determination by a maximum or minimum by that other, "that instead of the least, it is necessary to adhere to the *most determined*, which can be the *simplest*, even when it is the greatest" (p. 274). The equilateral triangle is a case of the most determined effect, since there are an infinity of different triangles of unequal sides, but only one equilateral triangle.

through the idea of a maximum takes place. Examples of this kind of determination occur in geometry where the right angle is the most determinate among all others;[5] or in physics, when one liquid put into another heterogenous one takes the shape of the maximum volume, namely of the sphere; or in ordinary mechanics itself, when the action of several competing heavy bodies tending downward eventually results in the motion producing the maximum descent.[6] For just as all possibles tend toward existence with the same right, but in proportion to their reality, so all weights tend toward falling downward with the same right, but in proportion to their gravity. And just as, in the case of the weights, that motion results which produces the greatest possible descent of weight, so also, in the case of the possible, that world emerges through which the maximum of possibles is produced into actuality.

Thus, we have already derived physical from metaphysical necessity: for though the world is not necessary, metaphysically speaking, so that the contrary would imply contradiction or logical absurdity, yet it is physically necessary, or determined in such a manner that the contrary would imply imperfection or moral absurdity. And just as possibility is the principle of essence, so perfection or degree of essence (through which the greatest number is made compossible) is the principle of existence. At the same time, this makes it evident that freedom must be attributed to the Author of the World, though he does everything in a manner which is determined: he acts according to the principle of wisdom, that is, perfection. Indifference, indeed, originates in ignorance, and the wiser anyone is, the more he is determined to choose the most perfect.

This comparison of some determinant metaphysical mechanism with the physical mechanism of heavy bodies—thus you

5 The right angle is again an example of a maximum of determination: there is only one right angle, and there is an infinity of oblique angles.

6 It must be remembered that the lowest point of the common center of gravity of a system of bodies lies between them (for example, that of a chain fixed at both ends). This principle had been established by Torricelli, *De motu gravium naturaliter descendentium* (*Opera geometrica*, Florence, 1644).

may object—may appear ingenious. Yet it is inadequate in that the downward-tending heavy bodies really exist, while the possibles or essences are imaginary or fictitious before, or independently of, existence; therefore no reason for existence can be drawn from them. To this I answer that neither those essences nor the so-called eternal truths about them are fictitious, but that they do exist, so to speak, in some region of ideas, namely in God himself, who is the source of all essences and of the existence of all that exists outside himself. This is not to be considered a groundless affirmation: it is confirmed by the actual existence of the series of states of the world. For it has been proved above that the reason for existence cannot be found in this series, but has to be looked for in metaphysical necessities or eternal truths; it has also been pointed out that existence can derive only from existence: hence the eternal truths must have existence in some absolutely, that is, metaphysically, necessary subject, namely in God by whom the possibles which otherwise would be imaginary are realized (if I may use a barbaric but significant expression).[7]

We observe, indeed, that everything that happens in the world follows the laws of the eternal truths, which belong not only to geometry, but equally to metaphysics. This means that whatever happens does so not only according to material necessities, but also according to formal reasons. This is true not only in general, when it is a question of explaining, as we have just done, why a world exists rather than no world, and why it is as it is and not different—a reason which certainly must be drawn from the tendency of all possibles toward actuality; it is equally true when we now step down to special cases. We shall then understand that everywhere in nature the metaphysical laws of cause, potency, and action apply in an admirable way and that they even prevail over the very laws of pure geometry which determine material processes. This I understood with great admiration when I tried to account for the laws of movement. Finally I was forced by this discovery to abandon the law of the

---

[7] In Latin, the word *realisare* is, in fact, a barbaric neologism.

geometrical composition of forces, which I had myself defended in my youth, when I thought more materialistically. But this I have explained in greater detail elsewhere.[8]

Thus we have found the ultimate reason for the reality of the essences as well as of the existences in a unique being, which is necessarily and incontestably greater than, superior to, and anterior to, the world, since to Him not only all existing things comprehended in the world but also the possibles owe their reality. This reality can emanate only from a single source, in view of the interconnection of all these possibles and existences. It is evident that the existing things continually emanate from this source, that they are being and have been produced by it, since there is no reason why any one state of the world rather than another, why yesterday's rather than today's, should flow from it. It becomes clear also how God acts according to laws of physics, yet freely; how he can be not only the efficient but also the final cause of the world; and how he not only manifests his greatness or power in the machine of the universe which is already working, but manifests also his goodness and wisdom in its construction.

Some might believe that I am here confounding moral perfection, that is, goodness, with metaphysical perfection, that is, greatness, and might concede the latter but deny the former. To avoid such a misinterpretation, the consequences of what has been proved must be kept in mind. Namely, not only that the world is physically or (if you prefer) metaphysically perfect— that is, that the series of things which has been produced offers the greatest possible sum total of actual reality—but that this world is also morally the most perfect, because moral perfection is indeed the natural perfection of minds. Hence the world is

---

[8] See the *Specimen dynamicum pro admirandis naturae legibus circa corporum vires et mutuas actiones detegendis et ad suas causas revocandis* (*A Dynamic Model for Discovering and Referring Back to Their Causes the Admirable Laws of Nature Governing the Forces and Mutual Actions of Bodies*) (*Mathematische Schriften*, Gerhardt edn., VI, 234) and the *Critical Remarks Concerning the General part of Descartes' Principles*, Part II, article 64 (p. 78 of this volume).

not only the most admirable machine, but in so far as it consists of minds, it is also the best Republic, that in which the minds are granted the greatest possible happiness and joy; for in this consists their natural perfection.

But experience in this world, you may object, shows us the contrary. For the best people often have the worst lives; innocents—not only beasts but also men—are cruelly afflicted with evils and even put to death; and finally, the world, particularly if we consider the government of the human race, looks like a confused chaos rather than like the well-ordered work of supreme wisdom. That *prima facie* this may be the impression you gain, I do not deny. But on closer inspection, the contrary must be stated. It is certain a priori, by the very reasons we have adduced, that all things, and especially minds, obtain the greatest possible perfection.

It is unjust indeed, as the jurists are wont to say, to judge before having studied the entire law. We know only an infinitesimally small part of the eternity which stretches out beyond measure, and the memory of a few thousand years which history preserves for us is of very little avail here. Yet from such small experience we cast judgment with temerity on the immense and eternal, behaving in this respect like men born and brought up in prison, or, if you prefer, in the underground salt mines of Sarmatia, who would believe that there is no other light in the world than that miserable lamp which hardly suffices to direct their steps. Let us view a very beautiful picture and then cover it up, leaving visible only a tiny particle of its surface. What else will then appear to us, even if we inspect it from very near— indeed, the more so the nearer we get to it—what else will we see, but confused patches of colors without meaning and art? Yet, once you have removed the cover and contemplated the whole picture from a suitable distance, you will understand that what looked like color patches made at random has been created with art by the author of the work. What the eyes apprehend in a painting is apprehended by the ears in music. The greatest composers, indeed, are accustomed to mixing frequent dissonances among the consonances, in order to excite and to shock, so to speak, the auditor, who becomes anxious about what is going to happen; when after a short while all returns to order again, his pleasure will be so much more intense. Similarly, we enjoy insignificant dangers and painful experiences, because they give us the proud consciousness of our power and our happiness. Similarly also, when we see tight-rope walkers or sword dancers performing, we draw pleasure from our very shivers of fear. And frequently when playing with children, we laughingly pretend to throw and almost drop them. So it was that a female monkey once seized King Christian of Denmark, then still an infant in swaddling bands, and carried him to the top of the roof; then amid general anxiety the monkey—apparently enjoying the joke—carried him back, safe and sound, to his cradle. For the same reason one becomes tired of eating nothing but sweets; acrid, sour, even bitter ingredients have to be added to stimulate the taste. Who has not tasted bitter food does not deserve sweets and will not even appreciate them. This is the very law of pleasure, that uniformity does not allow it to continue with the same intensity, but produces satiety and dullness instead of enjoyment.

What we have just pointed out concerning disorder in certain parts, which may well be consistent with the harmony of the whole, should not be understood to mean that the parts were not taken into consideration at all, as though it sufficed that the world as a whole be perfect; for if this were so, the entire human race might be miserable. Nor does it mean that no care has been taken to safeguard justice or to protect our own interests. This, indeed, has been the opinion of certain authors whose judgment about the totality of things has not been sufficiently thought through. For it must be realized that in the best-constituted republic care is taken to grant everyone the greatest possible good, and that, analogously, the universe would not be sufficiently perfect unless the interest of everyone were taken into consideration, without prejudice, of course, to the harmony. There is no better verification of this than the very law of justice which ordains that each one should have his share in the perfection of the universe, and that his happiness should be proportionate to his virtue and to his voluntary contribution to the common good; this is what we call charity and love of God, and in this alone consists also the essence and power of the Christian religion, according to the judgments of learned theologians. Nor should one be surprised that in the universe spirits are the objects of so much solicitude, since they most faithfully reflect the image of the Supreme Creator, and since their relation to him is not so much that of a machine to its artificer (as is the case with all other created things), as it is that of a citizen to his prince. Moreover, the spirits will last as long as the universe itself, and in a certain way they express the whole and concentrate it in themselves, so that we may well call them total parts.

With regard to the afflictions of good people, in particular, it may be considered certain that these will turn to their greater advantage. This is true not only theologically but also physically, as evidenced by the grain of wheat fallen into the ground, which must die before it can bring forth fruit.[9] In general it may be affirmed that afflictions are temporary evils leading to good effects, since they are shortcuts to greater perfection. Just so, in physics, liquids with slow fermentation also clarify more slowly, while those in which the disturbance is more violent eliminate certain particles with greater force and are thus clarified more promptly. It might be said of these evils that one steps back, the better to jump forward. What I have just said is not simply pleasing and comforting; it is truth itself. And in general, I believe that nothing is truer than happiness, nor anything pleasanter and happier than the truth.

As the climax of the universal beauty and perfection of God's works, it must also be recognized that the total universe is engaged in a perpetual and spontaneous progress, so that it always advances toward greater culture. Thus a large part of our earth is now cultivated, and this part will receive ever-growing extension. Though it is true that meanwhile certain parts may return to the state of wilderness or be again destroyed or deteriorated, this must be interpreted in the same manner which we proposed

9 John 12:24.

a while ago, concerning the afflictions of good people: namely, that this very destruction and deterioration promotes the future conquest of a greater good, so that the very damage turns, in a way, into profit.

To the possible objection that thus the world would of necessity have long ago turned into a paradise, it is easy to reply: Many substances already may have attained great perfection; yet, the continuum being infinitely divisible, there will always remain in the unfathomable depth of the universe some somnolent elements which are still to be awakened, developed, and improved—in a word, promoted to higher culture. This is why the end of progress can never be attained.

WHAT IS NATURE?
REFLECTIONS ON THE FORCE
INHERENT IN CREATED THINGS
AND ON THEIR ACTIONS

*To serve as a confirmation and illustration of the
author's Dynamics.*

1. Recently I received from the famous mathematician and
physicist Johann Christopher Sturm, the Apology, published
in Altdorf, for his dissertation *De idolo naturae*, which Gunther
Christopher Schelhammer, the eminent physician-in-chief in
Kiel, had attacked in his book *De natura*.[1] The same question
had occupied me long ago, and in my correspondence with the

[1] Johann Christopher Sturm, professor of physics and mathematics at
Altdorf (1635–1703) was one of the first German Cartesians. He developed
the doctrine of matter in the direction of occasionalism and, in physics,
attempted to reconcile it with the Aristotelian tradition. In 1686 he had
published a *Philosophia eclectica*, followed in 1697 by the first volume (the
second appeared only after his death) of the *Physica electiva sive hypothetica*
(Nuremberg). His correspondence with Leibniz, unpublished except for a
single letter of Leibniz published by Erdmann, I, 145, has been preserved
at Hanover. The discussion on the meaning and utility of the term nature,
already brought up by Descartes (Adam-Tannery, XI, 37) had been opened
again by Robert Boyle's book *De ipsa natura, sive libera in receptam naturae
notionem disquisitio (On Nature Itself, or a Free Inquiry Into the Received
Notion of Nature*, London, 1687), to which Leibniz alludes and which
had been defended by Sturm in *Idolum naturae . . . , sive de natura agentis
aliorumque cognatorum . . . superstitiosis erroneisque conceptibus dissertatio
(The Idol of Nature, or a Dissertation on Superstitious and Erroneous Concepts of a Natural Agent and Other Related Things*, Altdorf, 1692). Gunther
Christopher Schelhammer (1649–1716) professor of medicine in Helmstadt,
in Jena, and after 1695, in Kiel, attacked this work of Sturm in a book
entitled *Natura sibi et medicis vindicata (Nature Vindicated, in Itself and
by Medicine*, 1697), to which Sturm replied in 1698 in the writing which
Leibniz here calls an Apology, or Apologetic Dissertation, and which was
entitled *De natura sibi incassum vindicata (Nature Self-Vindicated in Vain*).

95

well-known author of the dissertation just mentioned, a certain
difference of views has appeared, as he himself has done me the
honor of mentioning recently, putting on public record certain
details of our discussion, in his *Physica electiva* (Vol. I, Book I,
sec. 1, chap. 3, Epilog. §5, pp. 119–120). Hence I have been very
much interested in devoting my thoughts and attention to a
problem which in itself is highly important; and I consider it
necessary to explain more distinctly my position concerning
this problem—according to the principles which I have proposed frequently before—as well as the present state of the
whole question. Sturm's apologetic dissertation provides a good
opportunity for this purpose, I think, because we may suppose
that in it the author has collected the most relevant arguments
in a short and comprehensive form. As for the rest, I do not
wish to interfere with the controversy between the two great
men.

2. Two main problems, I think, are under discussion: Firstly,
in what does that nature which we are used to ascribe to the
universe consist? Sturm thinks that the attributes of nature
commonly agreed upon have a certain pagan odor. The second
problem is whether in the created things there resides a certain
force (ἐνέργεια) [*energeia*], which he seems to deny. As to the
first problem concerning *nature in itself*, we may investigate
what it is and what it is not; but my opinion coincides with his
conclusion, namely, that there is no soul of the universe. I also
grant that the admirable events which occur every day and of
which we are wont to say, with reason, that the work of nature
is the work of an intelligence, are not to be ascribed to some
created intelligences, endowed with wisdom and power proportionate to such great achievements. The whole of *nature*, I
would say, is *a perfect work of God's making*, and this so much
so that every natural machine—this is the true but rarely observed *difference between nature and art*—consists in its turn
of an infinity of organs, therefore evincing the infinite wisdom
and power of its creator and ruler. Hence the *omniscient heat*
of Hippocrates, the *Cholcodea*, that soul-giving principle of
Avicenna, the all-wise *formative force* of Scaliger and others,

and the *hylarchic principle* of Henry More[2] are, to my mind, in part impossible, and in part superfluous. I am satisfied with thinking that the machine of the universe is constructed with so much wisdom that all those admirable events are produced by its very operation and that the living beings in particular develop, I would hold, from a certain preformation. Hence I approve the author's rejection of the fictitious created nature which would be endowed with wisdom and would construct and direct the corporeal machines. But this does not imply, I think, nor is it reasonable to assert, that there is no created force at all inherent and acting in the world of things.

3. So much for what nature is not. Now let us look a bit more deeply into what that nature is which Aristotle defined quite well as *the principle of motion and rest*. I think, however, that this philosopher has used these words in too wide an acceptation, covering not only local motion and rest, but *change* in general and στάσιν [stasin] or persistence. This is also the reason—to repeat it here—why his definition of motion, though more obscure than is justified, is nevertheless not so inept as it appears to those who suppose that Aristotle wanted to define local motion exclusively. But after this digression, let us come back to our problem.

Robert Boyle, the eminent scientist and expert explorer of nature, has written a little book, *De ipsa natura,* of which the gist, if my memory is correct, amounts to stating that nature should be considered as the very *mechanism* of bodies. This we may accept as a first approach. But if the matter is to be examined with greater precision, it will be necessary to distinguish in mechanism itself the principles from the derivations. To explain a clockwork, for instance, it does not suffice to say that it is mechanically driven, unless you distinguish whether its movement is produced by a weight or by a spring. I have contended several times before that the origin of mechanism itself does not flow from the material principle alone nor from

2 The *hylarchic principle* is explained in the *Enchiridion metaphysicum* (*Handbook of Metaphysics*) of Henry More (1614–1687), chap. 13, scholium (*Opera omnia* [3 vols.; London, 1675–1679], I, 222).

mathematical reasons, but from a higher and, if I may say so, metaphysical source. This restriction will serve, I hope, to prevent the mechanical explanations of natural events from being abusively used to the prejudice of piety, as though they implied that matter can subsist by itself and that mechanism does not require any intelligence or spiritual substance.

4. Among many other proofs of this conception, a remarkable one is offered by the *foundation of the laws of nature:* this foundation must not be sought in the conservation of the same quantity of motion, as was generally believed hitherto, but rather in the necessary *conservation of active power,* and even of the *same motoric action.* Moreover, I have discovered that motoric action is admirably proportionate to active power. The estimation of motoric action is entirely different from that of the quantity of motion as conceived by the Cartesians. I have discussed this question with two of the foremost mathematicians, partly in letters and partly in published writings. One of them has surrendered completely to my doctrine; the other has reached the point at which, after long and careful examination, he has abandoned all his objections and candidly confessed that so far he has been unable to find a flaw in a demonstration I have proposed.[3] I find it so much more astonishing that the illustrious Sturm, explaining the laws of motion in the published part of his *Physica electiva,* has adopted the common opinion on this subject, as if it were beyond doubt. And yet he himself recognizes that it is based not on any demonstration, but only on a certain verisimilitude—repeating this again in his recent dissertation, chapter 3, §2. Perhaps he had written this before my contributions to the problem were published and later he may have lacked time to revise his writing or not thought about it. This is the more likely since he believes the laws of motion to be arbitrary, an opinion which I do not think entirely correct. For I believe that God has been determined by reasons of wisdom and order to give to nature those laws

[3] The two mathematicians are probably Huygens and Johann Bernoulli. It is known that Malebranche, also, agreed with the Leibnizian concept of the laws of motion and the shock of bodies.

which we observe in it. And from this appears what I pointed out years ago apropos of the Law of Optics—it was later fully approved by the famous Molineux in his Dioptrics—namely, that final causes are useful not only in ethics and natural theology for the advancement of virtue and piety, but even in physics itself for discovering and understanding recondite truths.[4] Since Sturm, when dealing in his *Physica eclectica*[5] with final causes, has relegated my opinion to the rank of hypothesis, I wish that he had examined it with sufficient attention in his final work. Certainly this would have provided him with an occasion to say many remarkable and religiously useful things on such an important and fecund topic.

5. Let us examine now what he himself says about the concept of nature in his apologetic dissertation and what still seems to be unsatisfactory in his explication. In chapter 4, §§2, 3 and in many other passages he grants that the motions now going on occur *by virtue of the eternal law* enacted at one time by God, and soon afterward he calls that law an act of will and a *commandment*. And he affirms that there is no further need for new acts of will, still less for new efforts or new interventions (§3), rejecting as a false imputation made to him by his adversaries the idea that God moves the world as a carpenter his ax, or as the miller operates his mill, either stopping the water or letting it run on the wheel. But this explication does not at all seem sufficient to me. My question is whether that act of will or command or, if you prefer, that divine law enacted at one time has endowed the things with an *extrinsic denomination* only, or whether it has created in those things a sort of permanent impression. Schelhammer, a man distinguished by his judgment as much as by his experience, calls this impression an *inherent law* from which the active and the passive events in

---

[4] This law of optics is the principle that light rays always follow the easiest path. Leibniz explained it in the treatise *Unicum opticae, catoptricae et dioptricae principium* (see note 6, p. 31). The work of William Molyneux (1656–1698) which Leibniz cites here is the *Dioptrica nova*, London, 1692.

[5] Read *Electiva*. This title is obviously miswritten through an inattentive confusion of the titles of Sturm's two major works. (See note 1, p. 95.)

creatures ensue (though the creatures in which the law inheres have, for the most part, no knowledge of it). The first theory is maintained by the authors of the system of occasional causes, and principally by the very subtle Malebranche; the latter is more generally received and, in my opinion, very true.

6. For since that past commandment no longer exists, it cannot now produce any effect, unless at its time it has left behind itself a durable effect which still subsists and operates. To think differently is tantamount, I think, to renouncing all distinct explication of natural processes. For anything might follow anything else with equal justification, if that which is absent in time and space can operate here and now without interposed agent. It is therefore insufficient to say that God, creating the world in the beginning, has ordered that thereafter it should observe certain laws, if this is understood to imply that his initial will was so inefficient that the world was not affected by it and that no lasting effect was thereby produced. Indeed, it is incompatible with the divine power and will, which are pure and absolute, to maintain that God wills and that yet nothing be produced or changed thereby, that he always acts but never achieves anything, and that he never produces any accomplished work (ἀποτέλεσμα) [apotelesma]. Certainly, if no trace were impressed on created things by the divine order: *Let the earth bring forth*, and *Let the living creatures multiply*, if thereafter the world had moved as though no commandment had occurred, it would follow—since there has to be some connection, immediate or mediated, between cause and effect—either that nothing happens now in conformity to the commandment, or that this commandment operates in the present only and must be constantly renewed in the future. But this latter opinion is rightly rejected by the author. If, however, the law enacted by God has left some vestiges impressed in the things, and if these things are so constructed according to the commandment that they are able to fulfill the will of the legislator, then it must be recognized that these things contain inherent in them a certain efficacy, form, or force. It is this efficacy, form, or force which we are accustomed to call by the name of nature, and from this

nature the series of phenomena follows in conformity to the original commandment.

7. This inherent force can be conceived distinctly, though it cannot be explained by an appeal to imagination. Nor should it, any more than the nature of the soul, be explained by this means. For Force is among those things which are accessible not to imagination, but to understanding. Therefore, when the author of the apologetic dissertation demands (chapter 4, §6 an *imaginable* explanation of how the law inherent in bodies— though unknown to them—operates, I interpret this to mean that he asks for an intellectually understandable explanation. Otherwise he would seem to postulate that sounds be painted or colors heard. Moreover, if the difficulty in explaining something were a sufficient reason for rejecting it, such a principle would justify the opinion which, he claims (chapter 1, §2), is wrongly imputed to him, namely that he would rather maintain that nothing moves without the divine will, than to admit under the name of nature anything the essence of which is unknown to him. Hobbes and others might with equal right base themselves on the same principle when they pretend that all that is is corporeal, because they are convinced that nothing incorporeal can be distinctly explained and imaginably represented. The refutation of this theory consists precisely in pointing out that in bodies themselves inheres an active force which cannot be derived from anything that falls under the imagination. Simply to reject this force and to admit but a divine decree given once and for all, which has nonetheless neither affected the things nor left any trace in them—this interpretation is far from facilitating an explanation. It is, on the contrary, tantamount to the philosopher's resigning and cutting the Gordian knot with a sword. For the rest, an explication of the active force, more distinct and correct than that hitherto received, can be drawn from my Dynamics, which contains the true theory of the laws of nature and the correct estimation of motion.[6]

8. But if some defender of the new philosophy which intro-

[6] The *Specimen dynamicum*. . . . See note 8, p. 90.

duces the inertia and torpidity of created things should go so far as to deprive the commandments of God of all lasting effect and all future efficacy and should not hesitate to require of him ever renewed efforts (an opinion which Sturm is prudent enough to reject), such a theologian may see for himself how to reconcile his doctrine with the dignity of God. But he cannot be excused unless he offers good reasons for the assertion that the things themselves can endure for some time, while their attributes, which are what we call their nature, cannot last. It is reasonable, however, to admit that, just as the divine *fiat* has left something behind, namely the subsistent thing itself, so also the no less *miraculous* word *benediction*[7] has impressed upon the things the lasting tendency to produce their effects and the power to operate—a power from which the operation flows if nothing obstructs it. To this may be added a point which I have explained elsewhere, though it does not seem to have been sufficiently understood at large, namely, that the very substance of things consists in their force to act and to be acted upon. Hence it follows that lasting things cannot even be produced if it is impossible for the divine power to endow them with a certain force which will subsist in them for some time. To deny this power would imply that no created substance—in particular no soul—remains numerically identical, that God does not preserve anything, and that consequently all things are but evanescent and fleeting modifications of the one divine substance, phantoms, as it were, of the only lasting existence. It would come to the same to say that nature itself, that is, the substance of all things, is God—a doctrine of ill repute which a subtle but impious author recently has proposed to the world, or at least renewed.[8] If there were nothing incorporeal in the corporeal things, it would be justifiable indeed to say that they consist in a perpetual flux and have no substance whatever—a consequence which the Platonists correctly recognized long ago.

9. The *second question* asks whether there are good reasons to affirm that the created things act, in the proper sense of the

7 Genesis 1:28–30.
8 An allusion to Spinoza.

word. Once it has been understood that the nature inherent in created things is nothing but the force to act and to be acted upon, this question coincides with the first. For an action without a force that acts is impossible, and conversely, a power which can never be exercised is a vain word. But since act and power nevertheless are different things, the one temporary, the other permanent, let us examine this question separately, too. In this respect I must confess that I find considerable difficulty in Sturm's explication. For he denies that created things can be properly said to act by themselves. Yet, soon afterward he implicitly concedes that they act, rejecting the reproach that in his doctrine the created things appear like the ax swung by the carpenter. I am at a loss to draw from these affirmations anything distinct, and I do not see that he explains with sufficient clarity how far he diverges from generally received ideas, nor what distinct notion of action he has conceived. The current metaphysical controversies show that this notion is neither obvious nor easy to define. Insofar as I believe that I have well understood the notion of action, I think that this notion implies and confirms the most generally adopted philosophic principle that *all action is the action of an individual substance (actiones sunt suppositorum)*. This principle I believe to be so true, that its converse is true, too: that is to say, not only is all that acts an individual substance, but every individual substance acts without intermission. And this is true also for corporeal substances, in which no absolute rest can ever be found.

10. Let us now consider with a little more attention the doctrine of those who, properly speaking, deny to created things all veritable action. In the past this doctrine has been held by Robert Fludd, author of the *Philosophia Mosaica*,[9] and nowadays it is defended by some Cartesians who believe that the things do not act but that only God acts according to the things which present themselves and to their properties. Things, therefore, are not causes but only occasions: they can only receive but not produce or elicit any change. This doctrine has been pro-

9 See note 20, p. 79.

posed by Cordemoy, de la Forge, and other Cartesians, but in
particular by Malebranche,[10] who has granted it the benefit of
his sagacity and of his brilliant style. But, so far as I can see, no
solid reasons have been offered by anyone. One may push this
doctrine so far as to deny even *immanent actions* of substances,
but then it is so obviously unreasonable that it does not deserve
any further discussion. In his *Physica electiva* (Book I, sec. 1,
chapter 4, Epilog. §11, p. 176) Sturm rightly has rejected this
opinion and thus proved his circumspection. Can anyone doubt,
indeed, that our minds think and will, that many thoughts and
volitions are produced in ourselves by ourselves, spontaneously?
This not only would be tantamount to denying human freedom
and making God responsible for evil, it also would repudiate
the evidence provided by our innermost experience and consciousness, which convince us that we are responsible for what
those who think differently would impute to God. If, however,
we grant that our minds have the inherent force to produce
immanent actions or, which comes to the same, to act imma-
nently, it has to be granted also as a logical consequence that
the same force is inherent in other souls or forms or, if you so
prefer, in the natures of all substances. Some may suppose that
among all natural things of which we have knowledge, our
minds alone are active, that is, that the force of immanent or,
if I may say so, *vital* action is conjoined with intelligence. But
this assertion certainly cannot be the result of any rational argument nor be defended otherwise than against the truth. What
may be said concerning the *transient actions of created things*

[10] The occasionalist concept is expounded by Geraud de Cordemoy in
Le discernement du corps et de l'ame en six discours (*The Distinction of
the Body From the Soul, in Six Discourses*), Paris, 1666; by Louis de la Forge
in the *Traité de l'esprit de l'homme, de ses facultez et fonctions, et de son
union avec le corps. Suivant les Principes de René Descartes* (*Treatise on
the Spirit of Man, of Its Faculties and Functions, and of Its Union With
the Body. According to the Principles of René Descartes*), Paris, 1666. In
these two Cartesians, occasionalism is related almost exclusively to the
union of soul and body. As a general doctrine it has been developed by
Malebranche in the *Search After Truth*, particularly in Book VI, Part II,
chap. 3, and Clarification XV.

will be explained more suitably in another place, and in part I have already expounded it elsewhere:[11] namely, that the *interaction of substances* or monads has its cause not in an influx, but in a harmony created by divine preformation. Each monad while following its own inherent nature and laws adapts itself to all the others outside itself. In this also consists the *union of soul and body*.

11. That bodies in themselves are inert is, of course, true, if it is correctly understood. It means only that once a body be supposed to be at rest, it cannot possibly set itself in motion, nor let itself be moved by another body without opposing resistance. Nor can it spontaneously change the degree of velocity or the direction which it has acquired, nor let it be changed by another body easily and without resistance. Hence it must be granted that extension or what is purely geometrical in bodies, if nothing else is added, cannot be the source of action and motion. In fact, matter rather resists motion by what Kepler has aptly called its *natural inertia*. Thus matter is not indifferent to motion and rest, as the common opinion assumes, but to be put into motion requires an active force proportionate to its quantity. It is this passive force of resistance (which implies impenetrability and something more) which, I submit, constitutes the notion of *prime matter* or mass, which is everywhere the same in a body and proportional to its magnitude. I have shown, moreover, that from this conception ensue laws of motion which are very different from those obtained if one recognizes in bodies and matter itself nothing but extension and impenetrability. And just as in matter natural *inertia* opposes itself to *motion*, so also in the body itself and even in every substance inheres a natural *constancy* which opposes itself to *change*. However, this doctrine does not favor, but rather opposes, those who deny that created things can act. For as certain as it is that mat-

11 *Système nouveau de la nature et de la communication des substances, aussi bien que de l'union qu'il y a entre l'âme et le corps* (*A New System of Nature and of the Communication of Substances, As Well As of the Union of the Soul and the Body*), 1695 (*Philosophische Schriften*, Gerhardt edn., IV, 477–487).

ter does not start to move by itself, as certain it also is (and confirmed by conclusive experiments concerning the transmission
of motion from one moving body to another) that a body preserves the impetus once received and retains its *constant* velocity; that is, the body has a tendency to persevere in this same
series of change, once it has entered into it. All these activities
and entelechies cannot be modifications of the prime matter or
mass, which is essentially passive. Sturm himself has judiciously
acknowledged this, and I shall come back to it in the following
paragraph. Hence one must infer that in a corporeal substance
there must be located a *first entelechy*, a first capacity (πρῶτον
δεκτικὸν) [*prōton dektikon*] for action, as it were, namely, the
primitive moving force: this has to be added to extension (or
that which is merely geometrical) and mass (or that which is
merely material). And it acts constantly, though variously modified by the concurrence of other bodies and their tendencies
and impulsions. This same substantial principle is what is called
soul in living beings and *substantial form* in other corporeal
objects. In so far as it constitutes, joined to matter, a truly
unified substance, that is, a unit by itself *(unum per se)*, it is
what I call a Monad. Eliminate these genuine and real units,
and you will have only beings which are but aggregates and,
consequently, bodies will not be real beings at all. For although
there are atoms of substance, namely our Monads which lack
parts, there are no atoms of mass or of minimum extension as
the ultimate elements, since the continuum is not composed
of points. Neither, of course, is there a being endowed with a
maximum mass or infinite extension, though there are always
some beings larger than others. There exists, however, one being which is the greatest by degree of perfection, that is, a being
of infinite power.

12. I see, however, that Sturm, in this same apologetic dissertation (chapter 4, §7 ff.), has devised certain arguments to attack the moving force inherent in bodies. *I shall propose abun-
dant reasons*, he writes, *to show that the corporeal substance
cannot possibly have any ACTIVELY moving power.* I cannot
understand, though, what could be a power not actively moving.

Two arguments, he continues, will demonstrate his contention: the one derived from the nature of matter and body, the other, from the nature of motion. The first can be summarized as follows: Matter is naturally and essentially a passive substance. Hence it is just as impossible to endow it with an active force, as it is impossible that God would wish to endow a stone, while it remains a stone, with life and reason, that is, to make it a non-stone. Moreover, all the qualities of bodies are but modifications of matter. Now, the modifications of an essentially passive thing cannot render it active (which is well said, I agree). But the traditional as well as the true philosophies will not find it difficult to answer. A distinction has to be made between *prime matter* and *secondary matter*. Secondary matter is a complete substance, but not merely passive. Prime matter is merely passive, but not a complete substance: to it must be added a soul or a form analogous to a soul, a first entelechy (ἐντελέχειαν τὴν πρώτην) [*entelecheian tên prōtên*] that is, a certain tendency or primitive power of action, which is the law inherent in this substance, impressed on it by divine decree. This doctrine will not be repudiated, I hope, by our famous and ingenious author. For recently he himself has maintained that the body consists of matter and spirit, which is correct, provided *spirit* is not conceived as intelligence (as it usually is), but as a soul or soul-like form, nor as a simple modification, but as that constitutive and persevering substance which I am wont to call a Monad and which possesses a sort of perception and appetition. This doctrine, which is well established and compatible with the benevolently understood theory of the Schoolmen, would have to be refuted before the argument of our author could be conceded any validity. Hence it also becomes evident that it is impossible to grant his presupposition, namely that all that is in the corporeal substance is a modification of matter. For according to the traditional philosophy, as is well known, there are souls in the bodies of the living beings and these souls are by no means modifications of those bodies. It is true that our eminent author seems to affirm the contrary and to refuse to admit that beasts have any kind of sensation, let alone soul. But he wrongly presupposes this as a premise of his demonstration, without having demonstrated it beforehand. As to myself, I think, on the contrary, that it is not consistent with either the order or the beauty or the reasonableness of the universe that only a very small part of matter should be endowed with some vital principle or immanent action. Greater perfection requires that all matter be thus animated. It is quite possible, on the contrary, that souls or at least soul-like forms are everywhere, although dominant and therefore intelligent souls, such as the human souls are, cannot be everywhere.

13. The *second argument*, which the eminent Sturm derives from the nature of motion is not, I think, any more conclusive. *Motion* is defined by him as nothing but the successive existence of the moving thing in various places. Let us grant this for the present, though it is not completely satisfactory and expresses the result of motion rather than its formal reason itself (to use the traditional vocabulary). Yet this definition does not exclude the moving force. For in the present moment of its motion, the body not only occupies a space commensurate with its size, it also has a conation or a tendency to change place, so that its next position follows by itself, by virtue of its nature, from the present. Otherwise the body *A* at the present moment (and therefore at any moment) of the motion would differ in no way from the body *B* which is at rest. It would also follow from the opinion of our author if, on this point, it is contrary to ours, that there is no means of distinguishing bodies from one another. For in the plenum there can be conceived no differentiation of the mass, in itself homogeneous, except that differentiation introduced through motion. The final result would be to assume that nothing ever changes in bodies and that everything always remains in the same condition. For let us suppose that one portion of matter does not differ from another of equal size and figure (which our author has to admit, since he refuses matter any active force, impulsion, and any other quality or modification besides its existence in a determined place and successively in other determined places): suppose, furthermore, that the condition of the body at one moment does not differ

from its condition at another moment otherwise than by the transportation of equal, congruous, and in every other respect identical, portions of matter. This being supposed, it becomes evident that the perpetual substitution of indistinguishable portions would make it absolutely impossible to discern in the corporeal world different conditions at different moments. The *denomination* by which one part of matter could be distinguished from another would be merely *extrinsic* and drawn from the future, namely from the fact that this part later will be in such-and-such other places. At the present moment, however, there is no difference whatever. Even the difference drawn from the future would be without foundation, because even in the future it will never be possible to state any actual and present difference. For there is no means of distinguishing one place from another nor one portion of matter from another occupying the same space, provided you assume that matter itself is perfectly homogeneous. It would be equally vain to have recourse to *figure* besides motion. For a perfectly homogeneous, undifferentiated, and continuous mass cannot receive any figure, that is, delimitation of diverse and distinguishable parts, except by motion itself. If, therefore, motion contains no means of distinguishing, it will not provide any such means for figures. And since all parts of matter which are substituted for others are perfectly equivalent, no observer, even though omniscient, would be able to state the slightest sign that a change has taken place. The condition would be the same as though no change and differentiation ever occurred in the corporeal world, and it would never be possible to account for the manifold appearances which we perceive. The situation would be the same if we imagined two concentric perfect spheres, perfectly similar to each other in all their parts and the one enclosed in the other in such a way that there is not the least space between them. If, then, we suppose either that the enclosed sphere rotates or that it is at rest, it will be impossible even for an angel, not to say more, to notice any difference between the states of this system at different times, or to find a means of deciding whether the enclosed sphere moves or is at rest, and if moving, according to what law. What is more, it would even be impossible to determine the limit of the spheres, since there is neither any interval nor any difference between them. Consequently, the very fact that any difference is lacking will make it impossible in this case to recognize any motion. This is why it must be accepted as certain (though those whose investigations of this problem have not been sufficiently thorough have not realized it) that such doctrines are alien to the nature and order of the universe and that *never and nowhere is any perfect similarity to be found* – which I think is among the most important of the new theorems I have discovered.[12] Hence it follows also that in nature there are neither corpuscles of perfect hardness nor fluids of greatest tenuousness, that is, subtle matter diffused throughout the universe, nor those ultimate elements which are adopted by some[13] under the name of first or second elements. Aristotle, whose profundity is underestimated by many, understood some of this, I think, when he taught that besides local change, alteration must be admitted, and that if matter is not to remain unchangeable, it cannot be everywhere the same. To account for this heterogeneity, that is, diversity of qualities and hence ἀλλοίωσις [*alloiōsis*] or alteration, which Aristotle has not sufficiently explained, we can refer to the various degrees and directions of the tendencies which are modifications inherent in the monads. This also makes it clear, I think, that something else must be assumed in bodies than a uniform mass, the mere displacement of which does not explain any change. Those who adopt the theory of *atoms* and *the void* introduce, of course, some diversity into matter, assuming it to be divisible at one point and indivisible at another, full in one place and with interstices in another. But once I had shed the prejudices of my youth, I found out long ago that the theory of atoms and the void has to be rejected.

The author adds that the continued existence of matter through time must be attributed to the divine will. Why then, he adds, should we not attribute to Him also what exists here

---

12 This is a reference to the principle of the identity of indiscernibles.
13 Descartes, *Principles*, Part III, article 52.

and now? To which I answer that this existence doubtless is due to Him, as is everything else in so far as it implies some perfection. But this first and universal cause which preserves all things, far from suppressing the natural subsistence of created things, on the contrary, grants them persevering existence once they have been created. Analogously, this same cause does not suppress the natural efficacy of a body once set in motion, but sustains its perseverance in an action once impressed upon it.

14. Many other points in the apologetic dissertation raise difficulties. In chapter 4, §11, for instance, the author discusses the problem of a ball transmitting its motion to another one through several interposed balls and comes to the conclusion that the last ball is set in motion by *the same force* which moved the first. It seems to me, on the contrary, that these two balls are moved by equivalent forces, but not by the same, since each one, astonishing as it may seem, is moved *by its own force*, that is, by its elastic force, compressed by the nearest ball and rebounding. (I do not discuss here the cause of this elasticity, nor do I deny that it has to be explained mechanically, namely by the motion of a fluid circulating inside the elastic body.) There is also reason to be surprised by what he asserts in §12, namely, that a body which is unable to set itself spontaneously into motion is equally unable to continue this motion by itself. It is true, on the contrary, that just as force is required to set a body in motion, so also, once it has received the impulse, no new force is needed to continue the motion, while force has to be expended to bring it to a stop. For the conservation by the universal cause, which created things need, has nothing to do with the present issue, and we have pointed out before that if this conservation abolished the efficacy of created things, it would also abolish their subsistence.

15. All this evinces again that the doctrine of occasional causes, which is defended by some philosophers, entails dangerous consequences, certainly against their intention, unless it is interpreted with certain restrictions, some of which are admitted by Sturm, while he probably will accept others later on. Far from enhancing the glory of God by abolishing the idol of

nature, this doctrine rather causes the created things to evanesce
into mere modifications of the unique divine substance, and it
appears to make of God, as Spinoza does, the very nature of
the universe. For whatever does not act, whatever lacks any
active force, what is divested of any discernible quality, and,
in one word, of all reason and foundation of its subsistence—
this can in no way be a substance. I am completely convinced
that Sturm, being a man outstanding in piety and learning, is
far from any such extravagances. Hence I have no doubt that
he will either prove conclusively that his doctrine is compatible
with the substantiality or even the diversification of things, or
that he will align himself on the side of the true doctrine.

16. For the rest I have many reasons to suspect that I have
not sufficiently understood his thought, nor he mine. Somewhere
he has conceded to me that some *particle of the divine power*
can, indeed must, be understood to inhere in the things as their
property or attribute, namely, I believe, some expression, imi-
tation or immediate effect of that power; for the divine power
itself cannot be divided into parts. One may refer, in this respect,
to what he once wrote to me and has repeated in his *Physica
electiva*, in the passage quoted at the beginning of this essay. If,
as it appears by his own words, the above has to be understood
in the sense in which we say that the soul is a particle of the
divine breath, then this point is no longer controversial between
us. I hesitate, however, to consider this as his thought, for I do
not see that anywhere else he teaches anything similar, nor that
he expounds what would follow from this opinion. I notice, on
the contrary, that the interpretation which runs through his
work is scarcely compatible with it and that his Apologetic Dissertation is entirely opposed to it. It is true that when he first
read my article on the force inherent in bodies, published in
the *Acta eruditorum* of Leipzig, March 1964 [14] (an article which
I have clarified subsequently in my *Dynamic Model* [*Specimen
dynamicum*], published in the same, April 1695),[15] he wrote

[14] *On the Improvement of Metaphysics, and on the Concept of Substance*
(pp. 81–83 of this volume).
[15] See note 8, p. 90.

me a letter proposing some objections. But soon afterward, having received my answer, he kindly declared that there was no real divergence between us, but only a verbal misunderstanding. However, when I examined the matter more carefully and pointed out to him some remaining divergences, he already had changed his opinion and stated several points on which we disagreed—which I admit. These controversial points were hardly eliminated when recently he came back to his former views and eventually wrote to me, claiming that there was no real, only a verbal difference between us, which I shall be glad to acknowledge. These are the reasons why, on the occasion of his newest work, the apologetic dissertation, I wished to formulate the issue in such a way that it should finally become possible to judge on the positions of both of us and to decide on which side truth stands. The ability of this excellent man in perspicacious research and lucid exposition is, for the rest, so great that from his continued effort some further light may be expected to be shed on this fundamental problem. The present discussion may, therefore, not remain useless if it offers him an occasion to expound and to clarify, with his usual painstaking power of judgment, some important aspects of the problem under discussion, hitherto neglected by the authors. As to myself, I am convinced that I have contributed to the solution of this problem through my discovery of some novel and most fundamental truths of wide scope. If I am not mistaken, some day these truths may engender a more correct and more adequate system of philosophy, equally distant from formalism and from materialism, but reconciling and preserving what is best in both.

A VINDICATION OF GOD'S JUSTICE
RECONCILED WITH HIS OTHER
PERFECTIONS AND ALL
HIS ACTIONS

1. The apologetic examination of the cause of God not only enhances the divine glory, but also serves our own advantage. It may move us to honor his greatness, that is, his power and wisdom, as well as to love his goodness and the perfections which derive from it, namely, his justice and holiness, and to imitate them as much as it is in our power. This apology contains two parts, of which the first may be considered as rather preparatory and the second as the principal. The first part studies, separately, *the greatness and the goodness of God;* the second, what pertains to these two perfections taken together, including the *providence* which he extends to all creatures, and the *government* which he exercises over the creatures endowed with intelligence, particularly in all matters concerning piety and salvation.

2. Theologians of excessive rigor have taken into account his greatness at the expense of his goodness, while those of greater laxity have done the opposite. True orthodoxy would consist in paying equal respect to both perfections. One may designate as *anthropomorphism* the error of those who neglect his greatness, and as *despotism* the error of those who disregard his goodness.

3. The *greatness of God* has to be studiously defended, particularly against the Socinians and some semi-Socinians, among whom Conrad Vorst[1] is in this respect the most reprehensible.

---

[1] Conrad Vorstius (1569–1620), professor of theology at Leyden, dismissed because of his theological opinions. His principal work is the *Tractatus theologicus de Deo, sive de natura et attributis Dei*, 1610. Like the majority of Socinians, he denied the foreknowledge of God, and particularly that He foresaw the acts of free creatures.

This greatness can be considered under two main headings, God's omnipotence and his omniscience.

4. The *omnipotence* implies God's independence from everything else, as well as the dependence of everything upon him.

5. The *independence of God* manifests itself in his existence as well as in his actions: in his existence since he is a necessary and eternal being and, as it is commonly expressed, an *Ens a se*. Hence it follows also that he is beyond measure.

6. In his actions he is independent both naturally and morally. He is naturally independent, since he is absolutely free, and determined to action only by himself. He is morally independent since he is ἀνυπεύθυνος [*anupeuthunos*], that is, has no superior.

7. The *dependence of everything on God* extends to all that is possible, that is, to all that does not imply contradiction, as well as to all that is actual.

8. The *possibility* of things, even of those that have no actual existence, has itself a reality founded in the divine existence. For if God did not exist, nothing would be possible, and the possibles are from eternity in the ideas of the divine intellect.

9. *Actual* beings depend upon God for their existence as well as for their actions, and depend not only upon his intellect but also upon his will. Their existence depends upon God, since all things have been freely created by God and are maintained in existence by him. There is a sound doctrine which teaches that this divine preservation in existence is a continued creation—comparable to the rays continually emitted by the sun—although the creatures do not emanate from the divine essence nor emanate necessarily.

10. *In their actions* all things depend upon God, since God concurs in their actions in so far as these actions have some degree of perfection, which must always come from God.

11. God's *concurrence* (even the ordinary, nonmiraculous, concurrence) is at the same time immediate and special. It is *immediate* since the effect depends upon God not only for the reason that its cause originates in God, but also for this other reason, that God concurs no less nor more indirectly in producing this effect than in producing its cause.

12. The concurrence is *special* because it aims not only at the existence of the thing and its actions, but also at the mode and qualities of this existence in so far as there is inherent in them some degree of perfection, which always flows from God, the father of light and dispenser of all good.

13. So far we have dealt with the divine power. Let us now proceed to his wisdom, which, because of its immensity, is called *omniscience*. Since this wisdom is the most perfect possible (just as is his omnipotence), it comprehends every idea and every truth, that is, everything, simple or complex, which can be an object of the understanding. It comprehends equally everything possible and everything actual.

14. His knowledge of the *possibles* constitutes what is called the *science of simple intelligence*. Its objects are the things as well as their relationships, and, in respect to both, their necessity or contingency.

15. *Contingent possibles* can be considered either separately or as all correlated in an infinity of entire possible worlds, each of which is perfectly known to God, though only one among them has been produced into existence. It is indeed useless to invent a plurality of actual worlds since a single universe comprehends for us the totality of created things in all times and places; in this sense we use here the term *world*.

16. His knowledge of actual things, that is, of the world produced into existence and of all past, present, and future states of the world, is called *science of vision*. It differs from the science of simple intelligence of this same world considered as merely possible only in that it contains, added to the latter, the reflexive knowledge whereby God knows his decree to produce it into actual existence. Nothing more is needed as a foundation for the divine foreknowledge.

17. The *science* commonly called intermediate is contained in the science of simple intelligence if the latter is taken in the sense we have expounded above. If, however, one wants a science midway between the science of simple intelligence and the science of vision one could conceive both the science of simple intelligence and the intermediate science differently from the

common usage. In this case one could assign to the intermediate science not only the knowledge of conditional future events but, generally, the knowledge of all contingent possibles. Thus the science of simple intelligence would be taken in a more restricted sense, namely, as dealing with possible and necessary truths, while the science of vision would deal with contingent and actual truths. The intermediate science and the science of simple intelligence would have this in common, that they both deal with possible truths, while the intermediate science and the science of vision would both deal with contingent truths.[2]

18. So far we have considered the divine greatness; now we shall deal with the *divine goodness*. Just as wisdom or knowledge of truth is a perfection of the understanding, so goodness or striving for the good is a perfection of the will. All will, indeed, has as its object the good, be it but an apparent good; but the divine will has no object which would not be both good and true.

19. We shall study, therefore, both the will and its object, namely, good and evil, which provide the reasons for willing and rejecting. As to the will, we will study its nature and its species.

20. The *nature* of the will requires *freedom*, which consists in this: that the voluntary action be spontaneous and deliberate, and therefore exclude that necessity which suppresses deliberation.

21. Freedom excludes *metaphysical necessity*, the opposite of which is impossible, that is, implies contradiction. However, it does not exclude *moral* necessity, the opposite of which is unfit. For although God cannot fall into error in choosing, and therefore always chooses what is most fitting, this is so little opposed

---

2 The distinction between the *science of simple intelligence* (*scientia simplicis intelligentiae*), the *intermediate science* (*scientia media*), and the *science of vision* (*scientia visionis*) was part of a system conceived, with a view to reconciling the foreknowledge of God with the free will of man, by the Spanish Jesuits of the sixteenth century (Molina, Fonseca, etc.). This doctrine had already been sketched by St. Thomas. For more details see the *Theodicy*, articles 39, 40, 102, and 103.

to his freedom that it rather renders it more perfect. It would be incompatible with his freedom if there were only one possible objective of the will, that is, if only one aspect of the universe were possible. For in this case there would no longer be any choice nor any possibility of praising the wisdom and goodness of Him who acts.

22. Therefore, those who maintain that only the actual—what God actually has chosen—is possible are mistaken, or at least express themselves awkwardly. This was the error of Diodorus the Stoic, according to Cicero,[3] and among Christian thinkers that of Abelard, Wycliff, and Hobbes. I shall deal with freedom more elaborately later on, when human freedom will have to be defended.

23. So much about the nature of will. We come now to the *division of will*. For our present purpose we must introduce two divisions: on the one hand, the distinction of antecedent will and consequent will, and, on the other hand, the distinction between productive and permissive will.

24. The *first division* distinguishes between acts of will which are antecedent or prior and those which are consequent or final; or, which comes to the same, the will either inclines or decrees. In the first case it is incomplete; in the second, complete or absolute. Some authors, however, explain differently this division (at least the first). They maintain that the antecedent will of God (for instance, that all men be saved) precedes the consideration of the actions of the creatures, while the consequent will (for instance, that some be damned) is posterior to this consideration. But the first also precedes and the second also follows other acts of the divine will. For the very consideration of the actions of the creatures is not only presupposed by certain acts of the divine will, but also presupposes in its turn certain acts of the divine will without which actions of the creatures could not occur. This is why St. Thomas, Scotus, and others understand this division in the same sense in which we do, namely, that the antecedent will is directed toward some par-

[3] Cicero, *Letters to His Friends* IX. 4. Compare Bayle, *Dictionary*, article "Chrysippe," and the *Theodicy*, articles 170 and 172.

ticular good in itself, in proportion to its degree of goodness, so that this will is only a relative will (*secundum quid*). The consequent will, on the contrary, aims at the whole and contains the ultimate determination whence it issues in an absolute decree. Since we are speaking of the divine will, it always obtains its full effect. For the rest, if anyone refuses to accept our explanation, we will not quarrel with him about words and if he prefers he may substitute for *antecedent* and *consequent, prior* and *final*.

25. The *antecedent will* is entirely serious and pure and ought not to be confused with velleity (which consists in this: that one would will if one were able, and would wish to be able), which does not exist in God; nor is it to be confused with conditional will, with which we do not deal here. The antecedent will of God tends toward actualizing all good and repelling all evil, as such, and in proportion to the degree of goodness and evil. How serious this will is, God himself confirmed when he so firmly asserted that he did not want the death of the sinner, that he wanted all men to be saved, and that he hated sin.

26. The *consequent will* arises from the concurrence of all antecedent acts of will. When the effects of all antecedent acts of will cannot be carried out together, the maximum effect which can be obtained by wisdom and power will be obtained. This will is also commonly called *decree*.

27. Hence it is evident that even the antecedent acts of will are not altogether vain, but have their own kind of efficacy. For though they produce effects, these effects are not always full, but are restricted by the concurrence of other antecedent acts of will. However, the decisive act of will, which results from all inclining acts of will, always produces its full effect, provided the power is adequate to the will, which it certainly is in the case of God. Only with regard to this decisive act of will is this axiom valid: who has the power and the will does what he wills. For since this power is supposed to imply also the knowledge required for action, nothing intrinsic or extrinsic can be thought of as lacking for action. And it can not be said that the felicity

and perfection of God *qua* will is in any way diminished by the fact that not all his acts of will produce their full effects. For he wills what is good only according to the degree of goodness which is inherent in it, and his will is the more satisfied the better the result obtained.

28. According to the *second division*, the will is either *productive* when it determines the actions of the agent himself, or *permissive* when it regards the actions of others. Sometimes one may permit (that is, not prevent) actions which one has not the right to commit, as for instance, acts of sin; on this, more later. The proper object of permissive will is not the permitted action but the permission itself.

29. So far we have dealt with the will; now we shall study the *reasons for willing*, namely, *good* and *evil*. Either of these is of three kinds: metaphysical, physical, and moral.

30. *Metaphysical* good or evil, in general, consists in the perfection or imperfection of all creatures, even those not endowed with intelligence. The heavenly Father, according to Christ's own words, takes care of the lilies of the field and of the sparrows; and according to Jonah, God watches over the animals.[4]

31. *Physical* good or evil is understood as applying especially to the advantage or disadvantage of intelligent substances. An example of this is the *evil of punishment*.

32. *Moral* good or evil is attributed to the virtuous or vicious actions of these substances, for example, the evil of guilt. In this sense physical evil ordinarily is the effect of moral evil, although the two do not always occur in the same subjects. This may seem to be devious, but the deviation is later redressed with such profit that even the innocents would not wish not to have suffered. See also below, article 55.

33. God wills what is good *per se*, at least antecedently. He wills in general the perfection of all things and particularly the felicity and virtue of all intelligent substances; and as has already been pointed out, he wills each good according to its degree of goodness.

---

4 Matthew 6:28–30, Matthew 10:29; Luke 12:6; Jonah 4:11.

34. Evils are not the object of God's antecedent will unless this will tends to suppress them. They are, however, though indirectly, the objects of his consequent will. For sometimes greater goods could not be obtained if these evils were eliminated. In this case the removal of the evil would evidently not produce the desired effect. Thus, though the suppression is consistent with the antecedent will, it is not taken over into the consequent will. This is why Thomas Aquinas, following St. Augustine, was right in saying that God permits certain evils to occur lest many goods be prevented.

35. Sometimes metaphysical and physical evils (e.g., imperfections in things and the evils of punishment in persons) become subsidiary goods, namely as means for greater goods.

36. Moral evil or the evil of guilt has never, however, the function of a means. For, as the Apostle admonishes, evil ought not to be done so that good may ensue.[5] At the most, moral evil sometimes has the function of the kind of condition called *sine qua non*, that is, of an indispensable and concomitant condition without which the desired good could not be obtained. For the desired good implies also the desired suppression of the evil. At any rate, the admission of some evil does not follow from the principle of absolute necessity, but from the principle of fitness. There must, indeed, be a reason for God to permit the evil rather than not to permit it; but no reason of the divine will can be determined by anything but the good.

37. Moreover, the evil of guilt is never the object of God's productive will, but only sometimes of his permissive will, since he himself never commits a sin, but, at the most, in certain cases permits it to be committed.

38. Concerning the permission to sin, there is a general rule common to God and man, namely, that nobody ought to permit another man to sin unless by preventing it he would himself commit an evil action. In one word, it is always *illicit* to permit another man to sin unless duty demands this permission. We shall elaborate on this below in article 66.

[5] Romans 3:8.

39. Thus, among the objectives of the divine will, the ultimate end is the best, while any good may be a subaltern end, and
indifferent events, such as the evil of punishment, may often be
means. But the evil of guilt is an end only as the condition *sine
qua non* for something which for other reasons ought to be. In
this sense, as Christ has said, "It is impossible but that offences
will come."[6]

40. So far we have dealt with the divine greatness and goodness separately, as far as is necessary for the preparatory part of
this apology. Now we shall study what pertains to the two perfections taken together. Now, *common to greatness and goodness* is everything which presupposes not goodness alone, but
also greatness (that is, wisdom and power). For greatness makes
it possible for goodness to attain its effect. Goodness, in its turn,
refers either to all created things or especially to intelligences.
Joined to greatness, goodness constitutes, in the first case, providence in the creation and government of the universe, and in
the second case, justice in ruling, particularly over the subter-
stances which are endowed with reason.

41. The divine wisdom directs the divine goodness which extends to the totality of created things. Therefore the *divine
providence* manifests itself in the total series of the universe.
It follows that among the infinite number of possible series God
has selected the best, and that consequently this best universe
is that which actually exists. For all things in the universe are
in mutual harmony and the truly wise will therefore never decide without having taken the whole into consideration, nor
will his judgment bear on anything but the whole. With regard
to the parts taken separately, the divine will may have been
antecedent; with regard to the whole, it must be understood
as a decree.

42. Hence, to speak rigorously, there is no necessity for a succession of divine decrees, but one may say that there has been
one decree of God only, which decree has produced into existence the present series of the universe, all the elements of this

6 Matthew 18:7; Luke 17:1.

series having been considered beforehand and compared with the elements entering into other series.

43. This is why the divine decree is also immutable, since all reasons which might be opposed to it have already been considered. But therefrom no other *necessity* arises than the necessity of the consequence, or the so-called *hypothetical* necessity. This is the kind of necessity which arises from the prevision and preordination attributed to God. This necessity is not absolute; it does not make that which follows (*consequens*) absolutely necessary, since another order of the universe was equally possible, both as to the parts and as to the whole, and since God by his choice of this contingent series has not abolished its contingency.

44. Despite the certainty of the events in this universe, our prayers and labors are not useless for the obtaining of those future goods which we desire. For when God contemplated in his mind the representation of this actual series before deciding to create it, this representation contained also the prayers which, if this series were chosen, would figure in it, just as the representation contained all the other causes of all the effects which the series would comprehend. These prayers and these other causes, therefore, have contributed their due weight to the choice of this series and of the events figuring in it. And the reasons which now move God to action or permission had already moved him at that time to decide how he would act and what he would permit.

45. We have already remarked above that events, though determined by the divine foreknowledge and providence, are not thereby determined absolutely to occur whatever you do or do not do, but that they are determined by their causes and reasons. Therefore, if one called prayers or effort and labor useless, he would indulge in that *Sophism* which the ancients already called *lazy*. See also below, articles 106 and 107.[7]

46. Thus the infinite wisdom of the Almighty allied with his

[7] This is the λόγος ἀργός cited by Cicero, *On Fate* 12. Compare *Theodicy*, article 55.

boundless goodness has brought it about that nothing better could have been created, everything taken into account, than what God has created. As a consequence all things are in perfect harmony and conspire in the most beautiful way: the formal causes or souls with the material causes or bodies, the efficient or natural causes with the final or moral causes, and the realm of grace with the realm of nature.

47. Whenever, therefore, some detail of the work of God appears to us reprehensible, we should judge that we do not know enough about it and that according to the wise who would understand it, nothing better could even be desired.

48. Hence it follows, furthermore, that there is no greater felicity than to serve so good a master, and that we should therefore love God above everything else and trust him without reservation.

49. The strongest reason for the choice of the best series of events (namely, our world) was Jesus Christ, God become Man, who as a creature represents the highest degree of perfection. He had, therefore, to be contained in that series, noblest among all, as a part, indeed the head, of the created universe. To him also all power has been granted in heaven and on earth, in him all the peoples were to be blessed, and through him every creature will be freed from servitude and corruption to enjoy the liberty and glory of the children of God.

50. So far we have dealt with general providence. Goodness, with special reference to intelligent creatures, together with wisdom, constitutes *justice*, of which the highest degree is *holiness*. Taken in this very wide sense, justice comprehends not only strict law but also equity, and therefore also laudable mercy.

51. Justice, taken in a general sense, can be divided into justice in a more *special* sense and holiness. *Justice in the special sense* is concerned with physical good and evil, namely, that of intelligent beings; holiness, with moral good and evil.

52. *Physical good and evil* occur in this life as well as in life hereafter. There is much complaint that *in this life* human nature is exposed to so many evils. Those who feel this way fail

to consider that a great part of this evil is the effect of human guilt. In fact, they do not recognize with sufficient gratitude the divine goods of which we are the beneficiaries, and pay more attention to our sufferings than to our blessings.

53. Others are particularly dissatisfied with the fact that physical good and evil are not distributed in proportion to moral good and evil, or in other words, that frequently the just are miserable while the unrighteous prosper.

54. To these complaints there are two answers: the first, given by the Apostle, namely, that the afflictions of this life are nothing compared with the future glory, which will be revealed to us.[8] The second, which Christ Himself has suggested, in an admirable parable: If the grain falling to the soil did not die, it would not bear fruit.[9]

55. Thus our afflictions not only will be largely compensated, but they will serve to increase our felicity. These evils are not only profitable, but indispensable. See also article 32.

56. A still greater difficulty arises with regard to *future life*. For there, too, it is objected, evil by far prevails over good, since few are elected. It is true that Origen has absolutely denied the eternity of damnation; some of the ancient authors, among them Prudentius,[10] have believed that only few would be damned for eternity. Some others have thought that eventually all Christians would be saved, and Jerome seems sometimes to have shared this opinion.

57. But there is no reason to resort to these paradoxes which are to be rejected. The true answer is that the whole amplitude of the celestial realm must not be evaluated according to our inadequate knowledge. For the Vision of God can give to the blessed such a glory that the sufferings of all the damned cannot

8 II Corinthians 4:17.

9 John 12:24.

10 Aurelius Clemens Prudentius, a Christian Latin poet of the fourth century, often mentioned by Leibniz. In the *Theodicy*, article 17, he quotes some verses by Prudentius on the subject of the small number of those who are eternally damned.

be compared to such a good. Moreover, the scripture acknowledges an incredible multitude of *blessed Angels*, and nature itself shows us a great *variety of creatures*, as new inventions[11] bring to evidence. Thus it is easier for us than it was for St. Augustine and other ancients to defend the predominance of good over evil.

58. Our earth, indeed, is but a satellite of one sun, and there are as many suns as there are fixed stars. Moreover, there is probably an immense space beyond all fixed stars. Nothing, therefore, prevents those suns and particularly the region beyond all suns, from being inhabited by blessed creatures. The planets themselves may be or become happy as Paradise. In our Father's house are many mansions, as Christ himself has rightly said of the heaven of the blessed.[12] Some theologians call that region the Empyreum and place it beyond the stars or suns, although nothing certain can be affirmed concerning the region of the blessed. Yet it may be affirmed that even in the visible world there are likely to be many mansions for rational creatures, without limitation of happiness.

59. Thus the argument drawn from the multitude of the damned is founded only on our ignorance and could be destroyed by one single answer, as hinted before: if all things were well known to us, it would clearly appear that a better world than that made by God could not even be desired. As to the penalties of the damned, they last on because the malice of the damned lasts on. An eminent theologian, Johann Fechtius,[13] in his excellent book on the state of the damned, has very well

11 The telescope and the microscope; see also below, article 143.

12 John 14:2.

13 Johann Fecht (1636–1716), professor of theology at Rostock: *Consideratio status damnatorum, quod actiones ipsorum, inprimis malas concernit,* 1680 and 1708. The justification of the eternity of suffering by the perseverance of the sinners in their wickedness had already been supported by St. Thomas. Compare, e.g., *Summa contra Gentiles* IV. 93: "Animae malorum post mortem habent voluntatem immutabilem in malo" ("After death the souls of the wicked have a will unchangeable in evil").

refuted those who deny that sins committed in the hereafter deserve punishment, as though the justice essential to God could ever cease.

60. The most serious difficulties, however, arise apropos of the *divine holiness*, that is, apropos of the perfection which refers to the moral good and evil of others. This perfection makes him love virtue and hate vice even in others and removes him as far as possible from pollution and contamination by sin. And yet, it is objected, crime is frequently triumphant in the midst of the realm of God Almighty. Yet, however great this difficulty, with the help of the divine light, it can be overcome even in this life so that the pious who love God can be satisfied in this respect as much as need be.

61. The *objection* points out, indeed, that God concurs too much in sin and man not enough. *God, it is said, concurs too much in moral evil*, both physically and morally, by his will, which produces and permits sin.

62. Those who hold this opinion observe that moral concurrence would take place even if God did not actively contribute to sin, since he permits or does not prevent it, though he could.

63. But, they add, God in fact concurs at the same time morally and physically because he does not only not prevent the sinners, but even helps them in a certain manner by providing for them forces and occasions. Hence the passages in the sacred Scriptures which say that God hardens and incites the evildoers.

64. This is the reason why certain authors even dare to infer that God is morally and physically, or certainly in at least one of the two ways, an accomplice, even the author, of sin. By this means they destroy the divine holiness as well as his justice and goodness.

65. Others prefer to tear down the divine omniscience and omnipotence or, in one word, his greatness. According to them, God either does not foresee the evil, or is not concerned with it at all, or is unable to resist its torrential flood. This was the opinion of the Epicureans and of the Manichaeans. Something

similar is taught, although in a less crude way, by the Socinians, who rightly wish to protect the divine holiness from pollution, but wrongly abandon the other divine perfections.

66. To respond first to the argument that *permission* is equivalent to *moral concurrence* we need only come back to what we have started to point out before, namely, that the permission to sin is legitimate (that is, morally possible) when it turns out to be a duty (that is, morally necessary). This is the case whenever another's sin cannot be prevented unless one commits an offense oneself, that is, unless one violates what one owes to oneself or to others. A soldier on duty, for instance, particularly in times of danger, ought not to desert his post with the purpose of preventing two friends preparing for a duel from fighting it out. See also article 36. If we speak of divine duties we understand this not in a human sense but Θεοπρεπῶς [*theoprepōs*] (as it is proper to God), namely, that otherwise he would act contrary to his perfections.

67. Furthermore, if God had not selected for creation the best series of the universe (in which sin does occur), he would have admitted something worse than all sin committed by creatures. For, in this case, he would have acted contrary to his own perfections, and thereby also to all other perfection. For divine perfection can never fail to select the most perfect, since what is less good implies some evil. God himself and with him all things would be abolished if God either lacked power, or erred in his intellect, or failed in his will.

68. The *physical concurrence in sin* is the reason why some authors have considered God as the cause and the author of sin. The evil of guilt would thus also be the object of God's productive will. The Epicureans and Manichaeans are most objectionable in this respect; but here again God himself, enlightening the mind, is, for pious souls who eagerly search for truth, his own defender. Hence we will explain how God concurs in what is positive in sin or in the part of evil which is good, but does not concur in sin formally.

69. Our reply, therefore, is this: In creatures and their good

or evil actions there is no perfection nor any purely positive reality which is not due to God. But in all actions of creatures which imply imperfection, this imperfection consists in a privation and originates in the original limitation of all creatures. This limitation is essential to them and is already inherent in their essence in the state of pure possibility, that is, in the region of eternal truth or of the ideas which offer themselves to the divine intellect. Indeed, a being exempt from limitation would not be a creature, but God. Every creature is limited in this sense, that its greatness, power, knowledge, and all its other perfections are limited or restricted. Thus the foundation of evil is necessary while its actualization is but contingent. In other words, it is necessary that evil be possible, but contingent that it be actual. What is not contingent passes from potentiality to actuality by virtue of the harmony of all things, that is, because of its fitness to figure in the series of the best, of which it is a part.

70. What we have affirmed concerning the privative nature of evil, following St. Augustine, St. Thomas, Lubinus,[14] and many other ancient and modern writers, is often considered futile or at least very obscure. I shall therefore offer an explanation drawn from the very nature of things which will base my opinion on a most solid foundation. Let us have recourse to the analogy of something sensible and material which also consists in a privation. Kepler, the outstanding investigator of nature, has used the expression *natural inertia of bodies* to designate what we refer to here.

71. Take the case (to use an easy example) of a river, carrying boats and communicating to them its own velocity, yet limited by their own inertia so that, all the rest being equal, the more heavily loaded will be carried more slowly. Hence it can

---

[14] St. Augustine, *City of God* XI. 9; XII. 7, 8; XIV. 14; *et passim*. St. Thomas, *De malo quaestiones disputatae* I. 1; *Summa contra Gentiles* III. 7. Eilhard Lubinus (1565–1621), professor at Rostock: *Phosphorus, de prima causa et natura mali.*

be stated that the speed of the boats comes from the river, the slowness, from the load; the positive, from the force of the propelling agent, the privative, from the inertia of the propelled.

72. Quite in the same manner it may be said that God contributes to the creatures their perfections, yet is limited by their receptivity. Thus all goods are due to the divine force; the evils, to the torpor of the creature.

73. This is why the understanding often falls into error through lack of attention and the will often weakens through lack of alertness. When this happens, the mind, instead of turning toward God as its supreme good, is drawn down through its inertia to the imperfection of a creature.

74. So far we have answered those who believe that God concurs too much in evil; now we shall satisfy those who say that *man does not concur enough*, or that he is not sufficiently guilty in sinning, so that the accusation again falls back on God. Our opponents attempt to prove this by the weakness of human nature as well as by the failure of divine grace to support our nature with the necessary help. We shall therefore consider in human nature both its corruption and the vestiges of the likeness of God which it has preserved from its state of innocence.

75. As to the *corruption of man*, we shall consider its origin and its nature. It has its origin in the fall of our first parents as well as in the hereditary transmission of the contagion. Of the *fall* we must again consider the cause and the nature.

76. The *cause of the fall*, namely, why man has fallen with God's knowledge, permission, and concurrence, must not be sought in some despotic power of God, as though justice and holiness were not divine attributes. This consequence would have to be admitted, indeed, if God were not concerned with right and equity.

77. Nor must the cause of the fall be sought in a certain indifference of God to good and evil, justice and injustice, as though these qualifications depended upon his arbitrary will. For if this were so it would follow that anything could have been constituted by him to bear these characters, and with

equal justice and reason, that is to say, with none.[15] This again would reduce all glory of his justice and his wisdom to naught, since he could find no joy in his actions nor any reason for joy.

78. Nor, finally, can the fall be explained by imagining the divine will to be neither holy nor worthy of being loved, thus representing God as if, interested solely in his greatness and glory and lacking goodness, he had created miserable creatures in order to have objects for his cruel commiseration; or as if by perverse justice he had created sinners to have creatures to punish. All this is tyrannical and completely alien to true glory and perfection—qualities which receive their splendor not only from his greatness, but equally from his goodness.

79. The true root of the fall, on the contrary, lies in the aboriginal imperfection and weakness of the creatures, which is the reason why sin has its place in the best possible series of events; of this we have already treated above. As a consequence, sin had to be permitted despite the divine power and wisdom; indeed, this permission could not be refused without prejudice to these perfections.

80. The *nature of the fall* must not be conceived of, as it is by Bayle,[16] in the sense that God, in punishment of Adam's sin, had condemned Adam and his posterity to continue to sin, and for the sake of carrying out this sentence had infused into Adam the inclination to sin (*peccaminositas*). In fact, this inclination follows from the first fall as if by a physical nexus, just as many other sins follow from intoxication.

81. We must now deal with the *hereditary transmission of the contagion*, engendered by the fall of our first parents and

[15] This opinion, that is to say, that God has established good and evil by an arbitrary decree, that things are therefore good because God has willed it so and not conversely, had been most strongly defended by Duns Scotus and William of Occam. According to Leibniz, the laws of justice, as well as the eternal truths, are "more inviolable than the Styx" and do not depend upon the will of God. Compare *Theodicy*, article 176.

[16] Bayle, *Réponse aux questions d'un provincial* (*Reply to the Questions of a Provincial*), chap. 178, article 3. Compare *Theodicy*, article 112.

passing from them into the souls of their posterity. There does not seem to be any more suitable explanation for this than to state that the souls of his posterity were already infected in Adam. To understand this doctrine, we must refer to recent observations and theories which seem to support the opinion that the formation of animals and plants does not proceed from some amorphous mass, but from a body which is already somewhat preformed, enveloped in the seed, and animated long before.[17] Hence, it follows that by virtue of the primeval divine benediction some organized rudiments of all living beings (and as far as animals are concerned, their forms also, however imperfect) and even their souls, in a certain way, were already existent in the first specimen of every genus to evolve in the course of time. But the souls and the principles of life which are in the seeds destined to be human bodies are supposed to run through a special process. They remain at the stage of sensitive nature, just as do the other seminal animalcules which have not that destination, until the time when an ultimate conception singles them out from the other animalcules. At the same time the organized body receives the shape of the human body and his soul is elevated to the degree of rationality (I do not decide here whether through an ordinary or an extraordinary operation of God).

82. Hence it also appears that I do not affirm the pre-existence of rationality. Yet one may believe that in the pre-existing germs there has been already prepared and pre-established by divine grace what at some future time is to issue therefrom, namely, not only the human organism, but also rationality itself, con-

[17] The theory of physical preformation—opposed to the epigeneticism of Descartes, who had said that in the germ cell there was only a "confused mixture of two fluids" (Adam-Tannery, XI, 253)—had been developed by Malebranche (*The Search After Truth*, Book I, chap. 6), following the microscopic discoveries of Malpighi and of Swammerdam. It was undoubtedly from Malebranche that Leibniz took the theory. For Malebranche, as for Leibniz, this theory is a means of explaining the transmission of original sin. There is, however, this essential difference between their theories: whereas for Malebranche it is only the body-machines which have been preformed since creation, for Leibniz it is also the souls.

tained in a sealed blueprint to be carried out later. One may also believe that the corruption of the soul induced by the fall of Adam, albeit this is not yet a human soul, attains the force of the original inclination to sin when later on it finally rises to the degree of rationality. From recent discoveries it appears, moreover, that life and the soul come from the father alone, while the mother in the act of conception contributes (under the form of the ovum, it is believed) only a sort of envelope and the food necessary for the full development of the new organic body.[18]

83. Thus we may overcome the philosophical difficulties engendered by the origin of forms and souls, and by the immateriality and, therefore, indivisibility of the soul, from which it follows that a soul cannot give birth to a soul.

84. At the same time we overcome the theological difficulties concerning the corruption of souls. For it can no longer be maintained that the pure rational soul—be this soul pre-existing or newly created—is introduced by God into a corrupt mass to be itself tainted by corruption.

85. Though we must thus admit a *tradux* (transmission of sin from generation to generation), it can be more acceptable than the one taught by St. Augustine and other eminent men. It will not be the transmission from soul to soul (which had already been rejected by the ancients, as is evident from Prudentius, and is, moreover, contrary to the nature of things), but it will be the transmission of life through a living being.[19]

86. So much about the cause of our *corruption;* now we shall treat of its *nature* and constitution. This corruption consists in original sin and in derivative sin. *Original sin* has such force that it renders men fragile in the body, and in the spirit dead

[18] The theory of physical preformation places the seeds, encased one inside the other, either in the maternal egg (*ovism*)—this is the opinion of Malebranche, Malpighi, Swammerdam, etc.—or, following the discovery of spermatozoa by Leeuwenhoek (1677), in the semen (*animalculism*). Leibniz here allies himself with the latter opinion. Compare *Theodicy*, article 91 and *Monadology*, articles 74 and 75.

[19] Compare *Theodicy*, articles 86–88 and 397.

until regeneration. It inclines the intelligence to sensible things and the will to things of the flesh. Hence we are by nature children of wrath.[20]

87. Pierre Bayle and other opponents who attack the divine benevolence, or at least obscure it by some of their objections, have affirmed that those who die corrupted only by original sin, before any opportunity for a sufficient use of reason and, therefore, before committing any actual sin (e.g., infants dying before baptism and those dying outside the Church), are of necessity damned to eternal hellfire. This doctrine cannot be admitted. It is preferable in such cases to commit these souls to divine mercy.

88. In this respect I approve the moderation of Johann Hulsemann, Johann Adam Osiander,[21] and some other theologians of the Confession of Augsburg, who eventually have become inclined to accept this same doctrine.

89. Furthermore, the sparks of the divine image, of which we shall treat soon, are not entirely extinguished. They can be stimulated again, by God's prevenient grace, to strive for spiritual things, and yet in such a way that grace alone effects the conversion.

90. Nor has original sin entirely alienated the corrupt mass of mankind from the universal benevolence of God. For though this world is steeped in evil, God nevertheless so loved it that he gave his only begotten Son for mankind.[22]

91. *Derivative sin* is twofold: actual and habitual. It is in these two forms that corruption manifests itself, so that it presents various degrees and kinds and contaminates our actions in various ways.

92. *Actual* sin consists in exclusively internal actions as well as in those which are both internal and external. It may be a sin of commission or a sin of omission. It may be a guiltiness engendered by the infirmity of our natures or a perversity engendered by the malice of our souls.

[20] Ephesians 2:3.
[21] Johann Hulsemann (1602–1661), professor at Leipzig; Johann Adam Osiander (1622–1697), professor at Tubingen.
[22] John 3:16.

93. *Habitual* sin originates in evil actions either frequently repeated or very violent, by reason of the great number or the depth of the impressions created by them. Thus malice, becoming a habit, increases the depravity which is due to original sin.

94. Though this bondage under sin spreads through the whole life of the unregenerated, it must not be extended so far as to think that no actions of the unregenerated ever could be genuinely virtuous nor even innocent, but that all of them always would be formally sinful.

95. Even the unregenerated may sometimes act in civic life through love of virtue and of the public welfare, motivated by sound reason and even by respect of God, without any mean consideration of ambition, private profit, or carnal passion.

96. Yet their actions always proceed from an infected source and contain an admixture of depravity (which, however, may be only habitual).

97. Yet, strong as man's corruption and depravity may be, they are not sufficient to render him excusable, nor to exempt him from culpability, as though he acted without sufficient freedom and spontaneity. There remain in man some *vestiges of the divine image*, which furnish the reason why God may punish sinners without prejudice to his justice.

98. The vestiges of the divine image consist in the innate light of reason as well as in the innate freedom of will. Both are necessary to render our actions virtuous or vicious: we must know and will what we are doing. It must be possible for us to abstain even from that sin which we actually are committing, if only a sufficiently strong effort were applied.

99. The *innate light* consists in simple ideas as well as in the complex notions which derive therefrom. Thus God and the eternal Divine Law are engraved in our hearts, although they are often obscured by human negligence and man's sensual appetites.

100. This innate light can be proved, against certain recent writers,[23] both by a reference to the Sacred Scripture which testifies that the Law of God is engraved in our hearts, and by

23 An allusion to John Locke.

rational argument, since the necessary truths can be demonstrated only by principles inherent in the mind, but not by induction from sensorial data. For it is never possible to infer universal necessity by induction from particulars.

101. *Freedom*, too, remains intact, however great the human corruption, so that man, albeit he doubtless is going to sin, is none the less never constrained by necessity to commit the sinful action which he is committing.

102. Freedom is exempt from both necessity and constraint. Neither the futurition of truths, nor the foreknowledge and preordination of God, nor the predisposition of the world renders our actions *necessary*.

103. *Futurition*[24] has not this affect; for although the truth of future contingents be determined, the objective certainty, that is, the infallible determination of truth, inherent in future contingents should not be confused with necessity.

104. Nor do the *foreknowledge* and *preordination* of God make our actions *necessary*, although they, too, are infallible. For God saw the events in the ideal series of possibles as they would come to pass, and in this series, also, man freely sinning. But in decreeing the existence of this series, he did not change the nature of things nor did he make necessary what in itself was contingent.

105. Nor does, finally, the *predisposition of the world*, that is, the various series of causes, involve a prejudice to freedom. For nothing ever happens for which the reason could not be given, nor do cases of indifference of equilibrium ever occur (which would be the case if, within a free substance and outside it, everything could be equal on one side and on the other). On the contrary, there are always, in the efficient cause and in the concurring causes, certain preparations which by some are called predeterminations. It must, however, be stated that these determinations are only inclining, not necessitating, so that a certain indifference or contingency always remains intact. The passion or appetite in us never is found to be so strong

---

24 Compare *Theodicy*, articles 36 and 37.

that our action follows from it with necessity. For as long as man has not lost his mind, he can always find some reason for arresting the impulse, however vehemently he be swayed by wrath, thirst, or similar causes. Sometimes it suffices in such cases that he remind himself to make the right use of his freedom and to exercise his power over his passions.

106. Predetermination, that is, predisposition by causes, thus is very far from introducing that necessity which we have explained and which is contrary to contingency, freedom, or morality. On the contrary, it is on this very point that the Mohammedan idea of fate is distinguished from the Christian, the absurd from the rational: the Turks are not concerned with causes while the Christians and all those who think rationally deduce effects from their causes.

107. It is said, indeed, of the Turks—I hesitate to believe, however, that all of them are lacking good sense to this point— that they think it vain to try to avoid the plague and similar evils, because they are convinced that the future events which have been decreed will occur, *whatever you do or do not do.* But this is false, since reason teaches us that he who unavoidably is to die of the plague, just as unavoidably will not escape the causes of the plague. For, as is rightly said in a German proverb, death wants a cause. The same is true for all other events. See also our article 45.

108. Nor are voluntary actions subject to *constraint.* For though the representation of external things has a powerful influence on our minds, our voluntary actions none the less are spontaneous, that is, have their principles in those who act. The theory of the pre-established harmony between body and mind, instituted by God from the beginning, is able to explain this more clearly than was hitherto possible.

109. So far we have dealt with the weakness of human nature. We turn now to the *help of divine grace,* which our opponents deny, thus again transferring culpability from man to God. There are two possible conceptions of grace: the first is the grace sufficient to him who wills; the second, that which produces the act of willing.

110. Nobody denies, it is true, the *grace sufficient for willing*. According to an old adage, to him who does what he can, the necessary grace is never lacking; and God abandons only those who abandon him, as St. Augustine himself has pointed out, following older authors. Sufficient grace is either ordinary, that is, dispensed through the Word and the sacraments, or extraordinary. The latter must be left to the divine discretion, as, for instance, that which He used toward St. Paul.

111. Many peoples never have received the doctrine of salvation of Jesus Christ, and yet it is not likely that his message will remain for ever without effect on all those whom it has not reached, Christ himself having affirmed the contrary concerning Sodom.[25] It does not follow with necessity, however, that anyone can be saved without the Christ, nor that anyone will be damned even though he has done all that is naturally in his power. For we know not all the ways of God, nor whether he will not, for extraordinary reasons, succor some at the very moment of death. At any rate, it has to be accepted as certain, and is evidenced by the example of Cornelius,[26] that those who have made good use of the light received, will also obtain the light they lack and have not yet received, although it may be granted to them only in the very moment of death.

112. The theologians of the Augsburg Confession recognize that the children of the faithful, who have been purified by baptism, are endowed with a certain faith, although it may be that no vestige of it is observed. For the same reason, it is quite possible that, to those mentioned in the preceding article, though they were not Christians before the moment of death, God may, by extraordinary means, at that very moment grant the necessary light which they lacked throughout their lives.

113. Thus, too, those outside the Church (οἱ ἔξω) [*hoi exō*], to whom only the external message has been denied, must be committed to the clemency and justice of the Creator, though we cannot know whom God will succor nor for what reason he will grant his grace.

25 Matthew 11:23, 24.

26 He was the first Gentile converted to the Christian faith (Acts of the Apostles 10:1).

114. But since it is certain, at least, that the *grace to will* is itself not granted to everybody, particularly not the grace crowned by a happy event, the enemies of truth use this argument to accuse God of hatred of mankind (misanthropy) or at least of partiality (prosopolepsy). They pretend that God is the cause of human misery, that he does not save all men, albeit he could, or that certainly he does not elect the worthy.

115. It is true indeed that if God had created the majority of mankind only to make his glorious justice triumph over their eternal malice and misery, neither his goodness, nor his wisdom, nor even his true justice could be extolled.

116. It is vain to reply that we are nothing before him, not more than the smallest worm is before us. In fact, this excuse would not diminish, but would increase, his cruelty. Indeed, God would be deprived of all love of mankind (philanthropy), if he cared no more for men than we for worms, for which we are neither able nor willing to care. In truth, there is nothing which escapes the divine providence by its smallness or embarrasses him by its multitude. He nourishes the sparrows, he loves man, providing food for the former and preparing felicity for the latter as much as depends upon him.

117. But if one should go so far as to contend that God's power is so boundless, his government so exempt of rules, that he has the right to damn even an innocent, this would render it difficult to attribute any meaning to divine justice. Such a Ruler of the Universe would deserve to be accused of *misanthropy* and tyranny and could not be distinguished from an Evil Principle, master of the universe.

118. It is evident that one still would have to fear such a God because of his power, but not to love him because of his goodness. For the actions of a tyrant certainly inspire not love but hatred, however great his power; indeed, the more so the greater the power, although the manifestations of hatred be stifled by fear.

119. Men adoring such a God and therefore imitating him would be driven away from charity to hardness and cruelty. Hence some authors wrongly have attributed to God, under the pretense of his absolute right, such actions as they would have

to recognize as highly blamable if committed by a man. Certain authors even have imprudently affirmed that what would be ignoble if done by others, would not be so if done by God, because he is not bound by any law.

120. Reason, piety, and God himself command us to think very differently of God. His supreme wisdom, allied with the greatest goodness, makes him fully observe the laws of justice, equity, and virtue. These perfections induce him to take care of all his creatures, but especially of those endowed with intelligence, whom he has made in his image, to produce as much felicity and virtue as the idea of the best world can contain, and to admit no vice or misery which it would have been possible to exclude from the best series.

121. Though it be true that before the infinite God we appear as nothing, it is precisely a privilege of his infinite wisdom to be able to take perfect care of what is infinitely below him. Certainly there is no assignable proportion between the creatures and God; nevertheless, they keep certain proportions among themselves and tend toward the order which God has instituted.

122. In this respect the geometricians imitate God in a way by the new infinitesimal analysis: from the relations which infinitely small and unassignable magnitudes have among themselves they draw conclusions concerning assignable magnitudes, conclusions which are more important and useful than one might believe.

123. Let us then reject that odious misanthropy and rightly support God's supreme *philanthropy:* He ardently wished all men to attain the knowledge of truth, all men to convert themselves from sin to virtue, and has evidenced this will by the frequent and manifold operations of his helping grace. If the objectives of this will have not always been attained, the responsibility rests with refractory human malice.

124. Yet, you might object, to overcome this resistance would not have been beyond his supreme power. I agree, adding however, that no law obliged him to do so, nor did reason otherwise demand it.

125. Yet, you will insist, the great benevolence which we rightly attribute to God might have gone beyond what he was bound to provide: indeed, the supremely good God was bound, by the very goodness of his nature, to provide the best possible.

126. At this point we must resort, with Saint Paul, to the treasures of supreme wisdom,[27] which absolutely has not allowed God to do violence to the order and nature of the universe, disregarding law and measure, nor to disturb the universal harmony, nor to select another but the best series of events. Now, in this series it was included that all men should be abandoned to their freedom, and some among them, therefore, to their depravity. The very fact that this is what actually happened confirms our conclusion. See also article 142.

127. At any rate, God's universal philanthropy, that is, his will to save all men, is evinced by the divine acts of help themselves, which suffice to all, even the reprobate, nay, are very frequently granted in abundance, although grace does not triumph in all men.

128. Moreover, I do not see why grace, in the cases where it attains its full effect, should attain it always by virtue of its own nature, that is, be effective by itself. It may happen, indeed, that the same measure of grace which does not obtain its effect in one man, because of his refractoriness or other circumstances, does obtain it in another man. Nor do I see any more how, on the basis of reason or revelation, it could be proved that victorious grace is always sufficiently powerful to overcome any resistance, however strong, and the most unfavorable circumstances. It does not behoove the wise to apply superfluous forces.

129. I do not deny, however, that in some cases God makes his grace triumph against the greatest obstacles and the most vehement obstinacy to convince us never to despair of anyone. But this should not be construed as a rule.

130. Much graver is the error of those who restrict to the elect the privileges of grace, faith, justification, and regeneration, as though all the temporary believers (πρόσκαιροι) [proskai-

<hr/>

[27] Colossians 2:3.

roi] were hypocrites—which is contrary to experience—and could receive no spiritual help from baptism, from the Eucharist, in general, from neither the Word nor the sacraments. This erroneous doctrine also would imply that no elect, once he is truly justified, could relapse into crime or deliberate sin; or again—a doctrine preferred by others—that the elect, even when plunged in crime, could not lose the grace of regeneration. The same theologians are wont to require of the faithful the firmest conviction that faith will stay with him unto death, while they deny that faith can impose itself on the reprobate and affirm that the reprobate are doomed to false beliefs.[28]

131. But this doctrine—which, if taken rigorously is purely arbitrary, lacks any foundation, and is entirely alien to the beliefs of the early Church and of St. Augustine himself—could influence religious practice. Even the wicked might draw therefrom the temerarious persuasion of their future salvation, while in the pious it might engender doubt and anxiety concerning their actual state of grace. Hence, a twofold danger: too much security for the former, too much despair for the latter. This is why, next to *despotism*, I care to fight this kind of "particularism" most energetically.

132. Fortunately it can be stated that a majority of theologians mitigate the rigorism of such a new and paradoxical doctrine and that the remaining partisans of so dangerous a teaching confine themselves to a merely theoretical position and do not indulge in practice in its odious consequences. The most pious among them work with filial respect and loving confidence on their salvation, inspired by a better Christian doctrine.

133. As to ourselves, we can be assured of our actual faith, grace, and justification, since we are aware of what is present in our consciousness. We also have good hope of our future perseverance, although mixed with some apprehension. For the Apostle himself has warned us: Let him that thinketh he stand-

---

[28] This paragraph summarizes the viewpoint on predestination held by orthodox Calvinism—an intransigent orthodoxy which Leibniz had fought on this point, in his attempts to unite the Lutheran and the Reformed Churches.

eth take heed lest he fall.[29] But the conviction of our election should never induce us to slacken in our pious zeal, nor to rely on our future repentance.[30]

134. The foregoing may suffice against the misanthropy imputed to God. Now it must be shown that it is equally wrong to accuse God of *prosopolepsy* (partiality, favoritism), as though his decree of election lacked reasons. The foundation of election is Jesus Christ; but that some men participate in the Christ to a lesser degree, has its cause in their own final wickedness which God has foreseen and reproved.

135. Here again we may ask why the divine means of succor—internal or at least external—are diversely granted to diverse persons, triumphing over wickedness in the one and vanquished by it in others. On this point, the doctrines are divided. Some think that God grants greater help to the less evil or at least to those who will resist grace with less obstinacy. Others maintain that the same help is more efficient in the former. Others, on the contrary, do not admit that certain persons are distinguished before God by the privilege of better, or in any case at least less evil, natures.

136. Of course, among the reasons for any selection made by the wise, there is undoubtedly the consideration of the qualities of the object. But it is not always the superiority of the object, taken absolutely, which constitutes the reason for selection. Frequently the fitness of the object for a certain purpose, given a certain set of conditions, will bear a greater weight.

137. Thus it may happen that for a construction or a decoration one will not select the most beautiful or the most precious stone, but the one which fits best into the empty space.

138. The most certain statement to be made in this respect is that all men, being spiritually dead, are equally evil, but not all in the same way. They differ by their depraved inclinations, and it may happen that those are preferred who encounter more

29 I Corinthians 10:12.

30 In this paragraph, it is the Lutheran Leibniz who speaks and who expresses the inward certainty of salvation (*innere Heilsgewissheit*) taught by Luther.

favorable conditions at their station in the universe, finding there less opportunity (eventually, at least) to manifest their peculiar vices and more to receive the sufficient grace.

139. Our theologians, too, have therefore learned from experience and recognized that the external helps to salvation create a very great difference between men, even though the internal grace be equal. Hence, to account for the economy of external circumstances which affect our lives, they have recourse to the βάθος [bathos] (profundity) of Saint Paul. For men are frequently either perverted or improved by the chances of birth, education, social contacts, ways of life, and even by fortuitous occurrences.

140. Thus we may understand that besides the Christ and the foreseen ultimate perseverance in the state of salvation, through which a Christian is devoted to him, no other foundation of election or of the gift of faith is known to us. Hence no rule ought to be established, the application of which we could understand, and which would allow us to flatter ourselves or to blame others.

141. God, indeed, sometimes vanquishes the worst wickedness and the most obstinate resistance, in order that no one should despair of his mercy, as Saint Paul has pointed out, alluding to himself. Sometimes even men of long-standing righteousness lapse midway, to prevent us from excessive self-confidence. Mostly, however, those who resist with less wickedness and strive more zealously for truth and goodness experience more completely the effect of divine grace, so that no one can believe that a person's conduct has no influence on his salvation. See also article 112.

142. But in the treasures of divine wisdom, that is, in the hidden God and (which comes to the same) in the universal harmony of the world, a profundity (βάθος) [bathos] is latent, which contains the reasons why the actual series of the universe, comprehending the events we admire and the judgments we worship, has been chosen by God as the best and as preferable to all others. See also article 126.

143. The theater of the corporeal world shows to us more and more of its beauty, even in this life and through the light of

nature, since the systems of the macrocosm and the microcosm have begun to be revealed by recent inventions.

144. But the most magnificent part of the world, the City of God, is a sight to which we shall at last be admitted some day, illumined by the light of the divine glory, to be able to know its beauty. For in our present state here below, this City is accessible only to the eyes of faith, that is, through absolute trust in the divine perfections. The better we understand that the City of God manifests not only the power and wisdom, but also the goodness of the Supreme Spirit, the more ardently will we love God and burn to imitate, as much as is in our power, the divine goodness and justice.

TABLE I

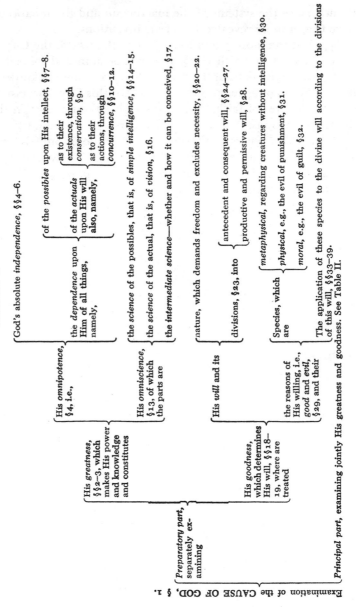

Examination of the CAUSE OF GOD, § 1.

- **Preparatory part,** separately examining
  - His *greatness,* §§2–3, which makes His power and knowledge and constitutes
    - His *omnipotence,* §4, i.e.,
      - the *dependence* upon Him of all things, namely,
        - of the *possibles* upon His intellect, §§7–8.
        - of the *actuals* upon His will also, namely,
          - as to their existence, through *conservation,* §9.
          - as to their actions, through *concurrence,* §§10–12.
    - His *omniscience,* §13, of which the parts are
      - the *science* of the possibles, that is, of *simple intelligence,* §§14–15.
      - the *science* of the actual, that is, of *vision,* §16.
      - the *intermediate science*—whether and how it can be conceived, §17.
  - His *goodness,* which determines His will, §§18–19, where are treated
    - His *will* and its
      - nature, which demands freedom and excludes necessity, §§20–22.
      - divisions, §23, into
        - antecedent and consequent will, §§24–27.
        - productive and permissive will, §28.
    - the reasons of His willing, i.e., *good* and *evil,* §29, and their
      - Species, which are
        - *metaphysical,* regarding creatures without intelligence, §30.
        - *physical,* e.g., the evil of punishment, §31.
        - *moral,* e.g., the evil of guilt, §32.
      - The application of these species to the divine will according to the divisions of this will, §§33–39.
- **Principal part,** examining jointly His greatness and goodness. See Table II.

TABLE II

- **Principal Part of the CAUSE OF GOD,** dealing with his greatness and goodness jointly, 40, in regard to
  - **all creatures in general:** *providence*, 41–49.
  - **intelligent creatures and their government,** 50; on God's
    - *justice in the narrower sense*, concerning physical good and evil of intelligent creatures, in this life and hereafter, 51–59.
    - *holiness*, concerning moral good and evil, 60–61, and the objections asserting
      - that God concurs too much in sin, i.e., in moral evil, 61–65,
        - *morally*, if only by permitting it; but this is shown to happen by reason of a higher moral necessity, 66–67.
        - *physically*, by cooperating; but this is shown to happen by reason of some good implied in evil, 68–73.
      - that man does not concur sufficiently, 74, because of defects in
        - his nature, in which have to be considered
          - its corruption, 76; its
            - cause:
              - the fall of our first parents; and again
                - its cause, with regard to { God, 76–78. man, 79.
                - its constitution, 80.
              - the transmission to posterity; also on the origin of the soul, 81–85.
            - constitution:
              - original sin (including the question of original sin as cause of damnation), 86–90.
              - derivative sin, 91, { actual, 92. habitual, 93–96.
          - the vestiges of integrity, 98, manifested in
            - the intellectual light, 98–100.
            - the free will, which is not suppressed; with refutations of objections, 101–108.
        - grace, 109, which is
          - *sufficient for willing*, given to all, but not refused in a higher degree { ordinary, 110. extraordinary, 111–113. to those who have made good use of the given degree of grace; it is
          - *efficient to will*, not given to all, 114, excluding
            - *misanthropy*, 115–127, including; when is the divine grace victorious by itself, 128–129; on the alleged restriction of God's grace to the few elect, 130–133.
            - *partiality*; treating of Christ as the reason of election, 134–138; in the ultimate reasons of particulars and in the economy of circumstances there must be acknowledged a βάθος, because in the universal harmony the consideration of the infinite is involved, 139–144.

MONADOLOGY

1. The object of this discourse, the *monad*, is nothing else than a simple substance, which enters into the composites; *simple* meaning, which has no parts.

2. And there must be simple substances, since there are composites; for the composite is nothing else than an accumulation or aggregate of the simples.

3. But where there are no parts, neither extension, nor figure, nor divisibility is possible. Thus, these monads are the veritable atoms of nature, and, in one word, the elements of all things.

4. Hence no dissolution is to be feared for them, and a simple substance cannot perish naturally in any conceivable manner.

5. For the same reason, no simple substance can come into being naturally, since it cannot be formed by composition.

6. Thus it may be maintained that monads cannot begin or end otherwise than instantaneously, that is, they can begin only by creation, and end only by annihilation; while what is complete begins and ends through and in its parts.

7. It is impossible also to explain how a monad can be altered, that is, internally changed, by any other creature. For there is nothing in it which might be transposed, nor can there be conceived in it any internal movement which could be excited, directed, or diminished. In composites this is possible, since the parts can interchange place. The monads have no windows through which anything could come in or go out.

8. Nevertheless, the monads must have some qualities, otherwise they would not even be beings. And if the simple substances did not differ through their qualities, there would be no means at all of perceiving any change in things. For what is in the composites can come only from the ingredient simples. So the monads, if they were without qualities, would be indistinguishable the one from the other, since they do not differ in quantity

either. The plenum being presupposed, no space, consequently, could ever receive through movement anything but the equivalent of what has been in it, and one state of things would be indiscernible from another.

9. Each monad must even be different from every other. For in nature there are never two beings which are perfectly like one another, and between which it would not be possible to find an internal difference, that is, a difference founded on an intrinsic denomination.

10. I take it also for granted that all created beings, consequently the created monads as well, are subject to change, and that this change is even continual in each one.

11. In consequence of what has been said, the natural changes of the monads must result from an *internal principle*, since no external cause could influence their interior.

12. But besides the principle of change, there must be a *particular trait of what is changing*, which produces, so to speak, the specification and variety of the simple substances.

13. This particular must comprehend a multiplicity in the unity, that is, in the simple. For since all natural change proceeds by degrees, something changes and something remains. Consequently, there must be in the simple substance a plurality of affections and relations, though it has no parts.

14. The passing state which comprehends and represents a multiplicity in the unity or simple substance is nothing but what is called *perception*; it must be clearly distinguished from apperception or consciousness, as will become clear later on. On this point the Cartesian doctrine has been very defective, since it has entirely neglected those perceptions which are not apperceived; the same failure to distinguish has made the Cartesians believe that only spirits are monads, and that there are neither animal souls nor other entelechies. Therefore, they, like the unlearned, have confused a long swoon with death, strictly speaking, and yielded to the scholastic prejudice that there are entirely separated souls. The same error has even confirmed unsound minds in the opinion that souls are mortal.

15. The action of the internal principle which produces

change, that is, the passage from one perception to another, may
be called *appetition*. It is true that appetition may not always
entirely attain the whole perception toward which it tends, but
it always obtains something and arrives at new perceptions.
16. We ourselves experience a multiplicity in the simple substance, when we observe that the least thought which we apperceive in ourselves comprehends a variety in its object. Thus, all
those who recognize that the soul is a simple substance must
recognize this multiplicity in the monad. Pierre Bayle should
not have found a difficulty in this theory, as he indeed did in
the article "Rorarius" of his *Dictionary*.

17. Moreover, it must be avowed that *perception* and what
depends upon it *cannot possibly be explained by mechanical
reasons*, that is, by figure and movement. Suppose that there be
a machine, the structure of which produces thinking, feeling,
and perceiving; imagine this machine enlarged but preserving
the same proportions, so that you could enter it as if it were a
mill. This being supposed, you might visit its inside; but what
would you observe there? Nothing but parts which push and
move each other, and never anything that could explain perception. This explanation must therefore be sought in the
simple substance, not in the composite, that is, in the machine.
However, there is nothing else to be found in the simple substance but perceptions and their changes. In this alone can consist all the *internal actions* of simple substances.

18. The name *entelechies* would fit all the simple substances
or created monads. For they have in themselves a certain perfection (ἔχουσι τὸ ἐντελές) [*echousi to enteles*], and they are endowed with a self-sufficiency (αὐτάρκεια) [*autarkeia*] which makes
them the sources of their own actions and, so to speak, incorporeal automata.

19. If we want to call *soul* all that has perception and appetition, in the general sense explained above, we might give the
name soul to all simple substances or created monads. But since
sensation is something more than a simple perception, I agree
that the general name monad or entelechy may suffice for those

simple substances which have nothing but perception and appetition; the name souls may then be reserved for those having perception that is more distinct and is accompanied by memory.

20. Indeed, we experience in ourselves a state in which we remember nothing and have no distinct perception at all, e.g., when we faint or are overcome by a deep and dreamless sleep. In this state the soul is not noticeably different from a simple monad. However, since this state does not last, the soul being able to pull itself out of it, the soul is more than a simple monad.

21. Besides, it does not follow at all that in such a state the simple substance entirely lacks perception. For the reasons propounded a while ago, this lack is not possible; for the monad cannot perish, nor can it subsist without some affection, which is nothing but its perception. But when there is a great multitude of minute perceptions lacking distinctness, one becomes dizzy: for example, when you turn around several consecutive times, you get a vertigo which may make you faint and leave you without any distinct perception. Death may throw animals into such a state for a time.

22. The present state of a simple substance is the natural result of its precedent state, so much so that the present is pregnant with the future.

23. Therefore, since on awakening from such a swoon, you apperceive your perceptions, it follows that you must have had some perceptions immediately before, though you did not apperceive them. For a perception cannot come naturally except from another perception, just as movement cannot come naturally except from another movement.

24. Hence it is evident that if in our perceptions there were nothing distinct nor anything, so to speak, in relief and of a more marked taste, we would always be in a swoon. And that is the state of the mere naked monads.

25. We see indeed that nature has given distinct perceptions to the animals, for care has been taken to provide them with organs which collect several light rays or several air waves, to unite them and thereby give them greater effect. Something

similar occurs in scent, taste, and touch, and perhaps in many other senses unknown to us. I shall explain soon how what occurs in the soul represents what occurs in the sense organs.

26. Memory provides the souls with a sort of *consistency* which imitates reason but has to be distinguished from it. For we see that animals, perceiving something which impresses them and of which they have previously had a resembling perception, are brought by the representation of their memory to expect what has been associated with this perception in the past and are moved to feelings similar to those they had then. If you show a stick to a dog, for instance, it remembers the pain caused by it and howls or runs away.

27. The vividness of the imagination which strikes and moves animals comes from either the strength or the frequency of preceding perceptions. For often one strong impression produces at once the effect of a long *habit* or of many reiterated impressions of minor strength.

28. Men act like animals in so far as the succession of their perceptions is brought about by the principle of memory. In this they resemble medical empiricists whose practice is not backed by theory. In fact, we are mere empiricists in three quarters of all our actions. If you expect, for instance, that the sun will rise tomorrow because up to now it has always happened, you act as an empiricist. The astronomer alone judges by reason.

29. Knowledge of necessary and eternal truths, however, distinguishes us from mere animals and grants us *reason* and the sciences, elevating us to the knowledge of ourselves and of God. This possession is what is called our reasonable soul or *spirit*.

30. By this knowledge of necessary truths and by the abstractions made possible through them, we also are raised to *acts of reflection* which enable us to think of the so-called *self* and to consider this or that to be in us. Thinking thus about ourselves, we think of being, substance, the simple and the composite, the immaterial, and even of God, conceiving what is limited in us as without limit in him. These acts of reflection furnish the principal objects of our reasoning.

31. Our reasoning is founded on two great principles: The first is the principle of *contradiction*, by virtue of which we consider as false what implies a contradiction and as true what is the opposite of the contradictory or false.

32. The second is the principle of *sufficient reason*, by virtue of which we hold that no fact can be true or existing and no statement truthful without a sufficient reason for its being so and not different; albeit these reasons most frequently must remain unknown to us.

33. There are also two kinds of *truths:* those of *reason*, which are necessary and of which the opposite is impossible, and those of *fact*, which are contingent and of which the opposite is possible. When a truth is necessary, the reasons for it can be found through analysis, that is, by resolving it into simpler ideas and truths until one comes to primitives.

34. Thus the mathematicians, using the analytical method, reduce the speculative *theorems* and the practical *canons* to *definitions, axioms,* and *postulates*.

35. In the end, there are *simple ideas* of which no definition can be given. Moreover, there are axioms and postulates, in short, *primitive principles*, which cannot be demonstrated and do not need demonstration. They are *identical propositions*, the opposite of which contains an express contradiction.

36. A *sufficient reason*, however, must also exist for *contingent truths* or *truths of fact*, that is, for the series of things comprehended in the universe of creatures. Here the resolution into particular reasons could be continued without limit; for the variety of natural things is immense, and bodies are infinitely divided. There is an infinity of figures and movements, past and present, which contribute to the efficient cause of my presently writing this. And there is an infinity of minute inclinations and dispositions of my soul, which contribute to the final cause of my writing.

37. Now, all of this detail implies previous or more particular contingents, each of which again stands in need of a similar analysis to be accounted for, so that nothing is gained by such an analysis. The sufficient or ultimate reason must therefore

exist outside the succession or series of contingent particulars, infinite though this series may be.

38. Consequently, the ultimate reason of all things must subsist in a necessary substance, in which all particular changes may exist only virtually as in its source: this substance is what we call *God*.

39. Now, this substance is the sufficient reason for all this particular existence which is, moreover, interconnected throughout. Hence, there is but one God, and this God suffices.

40. This Supreme Substance is unique, universal, and necessary. There is nothing existing apart from it which would be independent of it, and the existence of this being is a simple consequence of its possibility.[1] It follows that this substance does not admit of any limitation and must contain as much reality as is possible.

41. God, therefore, is absolutely perfect, *perfection* meaning the quantity of positive reality. In things which have limits, that is, in finite things, this perfection has to be strictly interpreted, namely as the quantity of positive reality within their given limits. But where there are no limits, namely in God, perfection is absolutely infinite.

42. It follows that creatures owe their perfections to the divine influence, but their imperfections to their proper nature, which is incapable of being without limits. For it is in this that they are distinguished from God. The created things' *original imperfection* manifests itself through the *natural inertia* of all bodies.

43. Moreover, it is true that in God is the source not only of all existence, but also of all essence endowed with reality, that is, the source of what is real in the possibles. For the divine understanding is the region of the eternal truths and of the ideas on which they depend, and without him there would not be anything real in the possibles; that is, without him there would not only be nothing existing, but even nothing possible.

44. Indeed, if there is to be any reality in the essences or possibles, that is, in the necessary truths, this reality must be

1 See below, article 45; see also p. 6 of this volume.

founded on the existence of the necessary being whose essence implies its existence, that is, to which it suffices to be possible in order to be actual.

45. Thus God alone (or the necessary being) has the privilege of existing necessarily, provided only he be possible. Now, since nothing can hinder the possibility of the substance which contains no limits, no negation, and hence no contradiction, this provides a sufficient reason for the knowledge a priori of God's existence. Besides, we have proved it by the reality of the eternal truths. In addition, we also have proved this existence a posteriori by the existence of contingent beings. For the sufficient and ultimate reason of these can lie only in the necessary being which has in itself the reason of its existence.

46. It must not be imagined, however, as certain authors have imagined, that since the eternal truths depend upon God, they are arbitrary and depend upon his will. Descartes seems to have thought so, and after him Poiret. This is true only of the contingent truths which are based on the principle of fitness, that is, the choice of the best possible; while the necessary truths depend only on his understanding, of which they are the internal object.

47. Thus God is the only primitive unit or the only original simple substance, of which all the created or derivative monads are the products, born, so to speak, every moment by continual fulgurations from the divinity, and limited by the capacities of creatures, to which limitation is essential.

48. In God there are his *power* which is the source of everything, his *knowledge* which contains the particulars of the ideas, and finally his *will* which is the source of change or production and acts according to the principle of the best possible. Corresponding to these divine attributes, there is in the created monads the subject or basis, namely, the faculty of perception and the faculty of appetition. In God, however, these attributes are absolutely infinite and perfect, whereas in the created monads or *entelechies* (Hermolaus Barbarus translated this word into Latin by *perfectihabies*) these attributes are only likenesses, possessed by the monads in proportion to their perfections.

49. Creatures are said to *act* outwardly in so far as they have

perfection, and to *suffer* from other creatures in so far as they are imperfect. Thus *activity* has to be attributed to the monad in so far as it has distinct perceptions, and passivity in so far as it has confused perceptions.

50. One creature is more perfect than another, in so far as there is found in the former a reason to account a priori for what is happening in the latter; this is why one says that the former acts upon the latter.

51. But in the simple substances this influence of one monad upon the other is but *ideal* and can take effect only through the intervention of God; in the ideas of God, indeed, any monad reasonably requires that in his ruling of all others, God, from the beginning, take that monad into consideration. For since no created monad can exercise a physical influence upon the interior of any other, this is the only means by which the one can depend upon the other.

52. By this means actions and passions among creatures are mutual. For when God compares two simple substances, he finds in either one reasons which oblige him to adjust the other to it. What appears as active in certain respects, consequently appears as passive from another point of view: it appears as *active* in so far as what is distinctly known in one monad serves to account for what happens in another; it appears as passive in so far as the reason for what happens in it is to be found in what is distinctly known in another.

53. Now, since in the divine ideas there is an infinity of possible universes of which only one can exist, the choice made by God must have a sufficient reason which determines him to the one rather than to another.

54. This reason can be found only in fitness, that is, in the degree of perfection contained in these worlds. For each possible has a right to claim existence in proportion to the perfection it involves. Thus nothing is entirely arbitrary.

55. This is the cause for the existence of the best, which is disclosed to him by his wisdom, determines his choice by his goodness, and is produced by his power.

56. This *connection* of all created things with every single one of them and their adaptation to every single one, as well as

the connection and adaptation of every single thing to all others, has the result that every single substance stands in relations which express all the others. Whence every single substance is a perpetual living mirror of the universe.

57. Just as the same city regarded from different sides offers quite different aspects, and thus appears multiplied *by the perspective*, so it also happens that the infinite multitude of simple substances creates the appearance of as many different universes. Yet they are but perspectives of a single universe, varied according to the *points of view*, which differ in each monad.

58. This is the means of obtaining the greatest possible variety, together with the greatest possible order; in other words, it is the means of obtaining as much perfection as possible.

59. Only by this hypothesis (which I dare to call demonstrated) can the greatness of God be exalted as it ought to be. Pierre Bayle has recognized this when he objected to the hypothesis in the article "Rorarius" of his *Dictionary*. In that passage he was inclined to believe that I attributed to God too much, and even more than is possible. But he was unable to adduce any reason why this universal harmony, due to which every substance exactly expresses all the others through the relations it has with them, should be impossible.

60. In what I have just stated, there can also be discerned reasons a priori why things could not be different. For God, legislating the whole, has considered every part and particularly every monad. And since the nature of every monad is representative, there is nothing which could limit it to representing only a part of all things. It is true, however, that this representation is but confused concerning the particulars of the whole universe and can be distinct concerning only a small part of all things, namely those which are either the nearest or the largest in respect to each of the monads. For otherwise every monad would be a deity. It is not in the objects of their knowledge, but in the modes of this knowledge that the monads are limited. All of them have a confused knowledge of the infinite, that is, of the whole; but they are limited and distinguished by the degrees of distinct perception.

61. The composite substances are in this respect symbols of

the simples. For since all is a plenum, all matter is connected and all movement in the plenum produces some effect on the distant bodies, in proportion to the distance. Hence every body is affected not only by those with which it is in contact, and thus feels in some way everything that happens to them; but through them it also feels those that touch the ones with which it is in immediate contact. Hence it follows that this communication extends over any distance whatever. Consequently, every body experiences everything that goes on in the universe, so much so that he who sees everything might read in any body what is happening anywhere, and even what has happened or will happen. He would be able to observe in the present what is remote in both time and space: σύμπνοια πάντα [sumpnoia panta], as Hippocrates stated. A soul, however, can read in itself only what is distinctly represented in it; it is unable to unfold all at once all its folds; for these go on into infinity.

62. Thus, every created monad represents the whole universe; nevertheless, it represents more distinctly the body which is particularly attached to it and of which it is the entelechy. And since this body expresses the whole universe through the interconnection of all the matter in the plenum, the soul, too, represents the whole universe by representing this body which in a particular manner belongs to it.

63. The body belonging to a monad which is its entelechy or its soul constitutes, together with this entelechy, what may be called a *living unit*, and together with this soul what may be called an *animal*. This body of a living being or of an animal is always an organism. For since every monad is, in its way, a mirror of the universe, and since the universe is ruled in a perfect order, there must also be an order in the representing, that is, in the perceptions of the soul, and consequently in the body. The representation of the universe in the body evinces this order.

64. Thus every body of a living being is a sort of divine machine or natural automaton, which infinitely surpasses all artificial automata. For a machine made by human art is not a machine in all its parts. The cog on a brass wheel, for instance,

has parts or fragments which for us are no longer artificial things, and are no longer proper to the machine with respect to the purpose for which the wheel was designed. The machines of nature (namely, the living bodies) are, on the contrary, machines even in their smallest parts without any limit. Herein lies the difference between nature and art, that is, between divine and human art.

65. The author of nature, indeed, has been able to practice this divine and infinitely marvellous art because any portion of matter is not only infinitely divisible, as the ancients recognized, but also actually subdivided *ad infinitum:* every part having parts each of which has its own particular movement. For otherwise it would be impossible for every portion of matter to express the whole universe.

66. Hence it can be seen that in the smallest portion of matter there is a world of creatures, living beings, animals, entelechies, and souls.

67. Thus every portion of matter can be conceived as a garden full of plants or as a pond full of fish. But every branch of the plant, every limb of the animal, every drop of its humors, is again such a garden or such a pond.

68. And though the soil and the air in the intervals between the plants of the garden is not a plant, nor the water between the fishes a fish, yet these intervals contain again plants or fishes. But these living beings most frequently are so minute that they remain imperceptible to us.

69. Thus there is nothing uncultured, sterile or dead in the universe, no chaos, no disorder, though this may be what appears. It would be about the same with a pond seen from a distance: you would perceive a confused movement, a squirming of fishes, if I may say so, without discerning the single fish.

70. Hence it becomes clear that every living body has a dominant entelechy which in an animal is its soul. But the limbs of this living body are full of other living beings, plants or animals, each of which again has its entelechy or its dominant soul.

71. But you must not imagine—like some authors who have misinterpreted my thought—that each soul has a mass or por-

tion of matter forever belonging or attached to it and that, consequently, it owns other living, though inferior, beings forever destined to serve it. For all bodies are, like rivers, in a perpetual flux; small parts enter and leave them continually.

72. Thus the soul changes its body bit by bit, and by degrees, so that it never is deprived all at once of all its organs; in animals there is frequently metamorphosis. Never, however, is there metempsychosis nor transmigration of souls. Nor are there any totally separate *souls*, nor *genii* without body. God alone is entirely bodiless.

73. This also proves that, strictly speaking, there never is either complete generation or perfect death, which would consist in the separation of the soul. What we call *generation* consists in developments and growths, just as what we call *death* consists in involutions and diminutions.

74. Philosophers formerly have been very perplexed concerning the origin of forms, entelechies, or souls. Today, however, it has been discovered through precise observations made on plants, insects, and animals that the organized bodies of nature are never produced out of a chaos or putrefaction, but always out of seeds, in which doubtless there has been some *preformation*. Hence it has been concluded, not only that the organized body was already in the seed before conception, but also that there was a soul in this body, and, in short, the animal itself. Through the conception, furthermore, the animal has only been disposed to a great transformation, namely to become an animal of a different species. Something similar can even be observed outside generation, as, for instance, when worms become flies, or caterpillars butterflies.[2]

75. Those animals among which some are elevated by means of the conception to the grade of larger animals, may be called *spermatic;* while those among them which remain within their species, that is, the majority, are born, multiply, and are destroyed like the large animals. Only a small number of elect pass on to a greater stage.

[2] See *A Vindication of God's Justice*, articles 81 and 82, and notes 17 and 18; see also below, article 82.

76. This, so far, has been but half the truth. Therefore I have concluded that if it be true that the animal never begins naturally, it will not end naturally either, and that consequently there will be, strictly speaking, neither generation nor entire destruction, that is, death. These arguments made a posteriori and drawn from experience agree perfectly with my principles deduced a priori a while ago.

77. Thus it may be said that not only the soul (mirror of an indestructible universe) is indestructible, but also that the animal itself is indestructible, albeit its machine often partly perishes, and casts off or takes on organic accretions.

78. These principles have enabled me to propose a natural explanation for the union or conformity of the soul and the organized body. The soul follows its own laws, and so does the body. They meet by virtue of the *pre-established harmony* prevailing among all substances, since they all are representations of one and the same universe.

79. The souls act according to the laws of final causes, through appetitions, ends, and means. The bodies act according to the laws of efficient causes, that is, of motion. And the two realms, that of efficient causes and that of final causes, are in mutual harmony.

80. Descartes has recognized that souls cannot impart force to bodies, because there is always the same quantity of force in matter. He believed, however, that the soul was able to change the directions of bodies. For at his time it was unknown yet that there is a law of nature according to which the total direction of matter is equally conserved. If he had been aware of this, he would have hit upon my system of pre-established harmony.

81. This system maintains that bodies act as though there were no souls (assuming the impossible); and that souls act as though there were no bodies; and that both act as though the one influenced the other.

82. As to *spirits* or reasonable souls, I find that essentially all the living beings and animals have the same nature, as I have said before, namely that the animal and the soul begin with

the world and end no more than the world. Nevertheless, the reasonable souls have this in particular, that their little spermatic animals have only ordinary or sensitive souls, as long as they remain undeveloped. As soon, however, as those who, so to speak, are elected attain human nature through an actual conception, their sensitive souls are promoted to the rank of human nature and to the prerogative of spirits.

83. Among other differences existing between ordinary souls and spirits, some of which I have already pointed out, there is also this one, that souls in general are living mirrors or images of the created universe, while the spirits are in addition the images of the Deity itself or of the author of nature himself. They are capable of knowing the system of the universe and of imitating some of it by architectonic specimens, each spirit being like a small deity in his field.

84. This is the reason why the spirits are capable of entering a kind of society with God, and why with respect to them he is not only as an inventor is to his machine (this being the relation of God to the other creatures), but also as a prince to his subjects and even as a father to his children.

85. Hence it may easily be concluded that the assemblage of all the spirits must compose the City of God, that is, the most perfect city possible, under the most perfect monarch possible.

86. This City of God, this truly universal monarchy, is a moral world within the natural world; it is among the works of God the most exalted and the most divine. In it consists veritably the glory of God: for he would be without glory unless his greatness and goodness were recognized and admired by the spirits. Properly speaking, his goodness is directed toward this divine City, while his wisdom and power manifest themselves everywhere.

87. We have established above the perfect harmony between two natural realms, that of efficient causes and the other of final causes. To this we must add here still another harmony, namely, between the physical realm of nature and the moral realm of grace, that is, between God considered as the architect of the machine of the universe, and God considered as the monarch of the divine city of the spirits.

88. This harmony has the result that events lead to grace through the very processes of nature, and that our globe, for instance, must be destroyed and repaired through natural processes at the moments when the government of the spirits so demands, to chastise some and to reward others.

89. One may add that God as the architect satisfies in all respects God as the legislator. Thus sin must entail punishment according to the order of nature and as the very result of the mechanical structure of the universe; and, analogously, good actions will attract their rewards through machinelike corporeal processes. Of course, these results cannot be and ought not always to be obtained as an immediate consequence.

90. Finally, under this perfect government, no good action will remain without its reward, no evil action without its punishment. All events in this city conspire to the advantage of the good people, that is, of those who are not discontented in this great State; who, once they have fulfilled their duties, trust in providence and duly love and imitate the author of all good; who enjoy the contemplation of his perfections as required by the nature of the true *pure love*, which consists in taking pleasure in the felicity of the beloved. This pure love makes the wise and virtuous people work at everything that seems conformable to the divine will, presumed or antecedent, and yet renders them contented with any event that God actually brings about through his secret, consequent, and decisive will. They realize that, could we only understand sufficiently the order of the universe, we should find that this order surpasses all the wishes of the wisest and that it is impossible to improve it; that it is the best not only for the whole in general, but also for ourselves in particular. For ourselves, that is, provided we are duly attached to the author of all things, not only as to the architect and efficient cause of our being, but also as to the master and to the final cause who ought to provide the sole goal of our will and who alone can give us happiness.